Los Angeles Times

SUNDAY MORNING, JUNE 6

Reviewers' Comments:

APPRAISERS, LAWYERS BOOSTED

Home Selling Guide Attacks Brokers

BY DAVID M. KINCHEN
Times Staff Writer

Most do-it-yourself home selling guides stress how you can save money by staying away from a real estate broker. A new book by Gerald M. Steiner does this and is also a lively-written attack on the entire system of residential brokerage.

His opinion of his fellow salesmen starts out low and goes downhill from there:

"Let me be the first to congratulate you on your wise decision to sell your home without the assistance of a real estate broker," he writes. "With the aid of this book, a knowledgeable real estate lawyer and an experienced local fee appraiser, you'll save approximately $3,000 on the sale of the average single-family residence."

If brokers won't like the book, fee appraisers and real estate lawyers should love it. Steiner has this to say about choosing a lawyer:

"If you don't have a good real estate lawyer in mind, do not call your local bar association for advice. They automatically lump the good with the bad and won't tell you the difference.

"All you have to do is call your local bank or savings and loan association; they will be happy to recommend several reputable attorneys who specialize in real estate."

Appraisers are important because Steiner, quite rightly, says that "overpricing accomplishes nothing and the over-priced home will not be in competition with similar homes currently for sale."

Steiner recommends that you ask your lawyer to find a good fee appraiser for you or select one who is a member of the Society of Real Estate Appraisers or one who is a member of the Appraisers Institute.

Steiner warns owner-sellers that they are literally asking for a real estate broker to pay them a visit the minute the house is advertised. This is a major source of listings for brokers, who don't just sit around waiting for people to come to them.

His advice: put a little sign on the front door reading "Real Estate Salesmen Not Welcome!!!"

"They (salesmen) know that if they solicit a home with such a sign they can be reported to the local police, the state real estate licensing bureau and the local real estate board," he says.

Even real estate brokers might want to obtain a copy of "Home For Sale by Owner" (Ana-Doug Publishing)

He certainly brings new meaning to Pogo's statement: "We have met the enemy and he is us!"

The Washington Post

Washington Post Co.   SATURDAY, JUNE 12   Phone (202) 223-6000

Housing in Print

Realty Salesman Attacks System

For sure, real estate brokers aren't going to like this book one bit.

Steiner is a suburban Chicago real estate salesman, at this writing. It may be that when "Home For Sale by Owner" (Ana-Doug Publishing, Chicago, Ill.) hits the bookstores, Steiner will join the ranks of the unemployed.

In a classic case of dirty pool, the author takes a study by the Florida Assn. of Realtors and uses it against them. The study examined home-sellers in Orlando and Gainesville who used brokers and those who didn't.

Of the sellers who sold through a broker, Steiner reports that the study showed that 72.5% of the sellers found the closing satisfactory, while 95% of the sellers who sold their houses themselves found the closing satisfactory.

Seventy-one per cent of the do-it-yourselfers did so because they thought brokers' commissions were "too high and unearned."

The study, called Project 6, "also uncovered the fact that there is a belief on the part of most buyers that a home being marketed through a broker is priced higher, by the amount of the commission."

That part of the book not given over to sample forms is devoted to a cram course in real estate.

Even real estate brokers might want to obtain a copy of this book from Steiner.

Chicago Tribune

THE WORLD'S GREATEST NEWSPAPER

Sunday, July 25,

How one sells his own home

Consumer watch
By Christine Winter

GERALD M. STEINER does not trust real estate salesmen.

That might not make him too terribly different from the average skeptic, except that Gerald M. Steiner is himself a real estate salesman—and the author of a book titled "Home for Sale by Owner." He published the book himself [Ana-Doug Publishing, Chicago, Ill.], and describes it as "the only complete home-selling kit."

It remains to be seen just how long he will remain employed in the field after his bosses and colleagues read his opinion of them and of the whole business of selling homes.

To set the pace, Steiner explains that he considers the residential real estate salesman "an anachronism," with "fees that are exorbitantly high" in relation to the services rendered.

"THE FUNCTIONS they perform can be accomplished more satisfactorily by lawyers, appraisers and bankers . . ." he maintains.

Thus, he sets out to guide the innocent homeowner on how to unload his own home, without pitching 7 per cent of the selling price over to the broker.

His first tip tells you how to shake off unwanted solicitation from brokers. A sign on the door saying "Real Estate Salesmen Not Welcome" means they can get in trouble with the local board if they continue to pester you, he said. He also cautions owners trying to sell their homes to beware of real estate salesmen who profess an interest in buying it themselves; they're just trying to set you up to sign with them, according to Steiner.

HE INSISTS THAT one of the most important steps is to get a full-time real estate lawyer, and to discuss fees with him beforehand.

Another major step in selling your house is pricing it right, and he warns against making the price too high. The best way to find the market value, he feels, is to hire a professional fee appraiser to come out and evaluate your home. The cost will be about $100.

Before taking your house off the market and marking it sold, Steiner suggests you try to talk the potential buyer into filling out a "confidential buyer qualification form" which gives you information on his salary, his credit rating, and his outstanding debts, so you have some idea whether or not he will appeal to a lending institution.

Steiner also advises you to get your house in good shape before showing it. The condition of your home is always disproportionately reflected in the sale price. If your home needs $1,000 in repair work, you'll have to drop your selling price by at least $3,000, he estimates.

"In all the years I've been selling real estate, I have never sold an 'open house.' Very few real estate salesmen have. When we hold an open house, we look upon it primarily as an opportunity to get prospective buyers."

The most likely prospects will be those who see your ad, or have come upon the "home information forms" that he urges you to print up and hang around your community. [These are a listing of all your house's amenities and vital statistics, similar to the listing sheets that real estate salesmen run off.]

CHICAGO Sunday Sun-Times

How to sell your home

Home For Sale By Owner

By Gerald M. Steiner. Ana-Doug

★★★★★

When the real estate market is as strong as it is today in many areas around Chicago, many people are tempted to handle the whole process of selling their home without the aid of a broker.

The saving if the home goes for the same price as with a broker is 6 to 8 per cent of the price of the house, less expenses.

Still, it's not a good idea to let a prospect drift around the house without accompaniment, according to Gerald M. Steiner, author of "Home for Sale by Owner."

"Be sure to listen to what the potential buyers has to say and never argue with him," Steiner advises. "If he says something foolish, just try to ignore it. Never talk down to a buyer—always try to meet him on common ground. Try to be patient with a buyer and be sure to avoid high-pressure tactics.

"Be enthusiastic when you're discussing your home, and this enthusiasm will be transmitted to the buyer. Make the buyer feel that your home is perfect for him and his family."

By far the biggest concern for the average seller is the legal problem of closing on the property. Some technical and legal considererations come into play at that point that scare off an otherwise d mined do-it-yourself seller.

"Most of the closing de should be handled by you torney. Legal fees usu amount to between one and 1 per cent, dependin the sale price. There is us a minimum fee, but to be discuss this with your atto prior to closing so that you know what amount will be ducted from the sale price his fee."

Otherwise, say home se who have done it themsel the main problems will c from persistent real estate kers trying to get a listing.

HOME FOR SALE BY OWNER

HOME FOR SALE BY OWNER

By

GERALD M. STEINER

Ana-Doug Publishing

4303 N. Bernard, Chicago, Illinois 60618

First Printing April 1976
Second Printing November 1976
Third Printing March 1977
Fourth Printing April 1978

Library of Congress Cataloging in Publication Data

Steiner, Gerald M. 1941 —

Home For Sale By Owner

1. House Selling   I. title

Library of Congress Number 76-9667

HD 1379.K67   333.3'3
ISBN 0-916946-00-2

DEDICATION

This book is dedicated to my father, William A. Steiner. He was always disturbed when he saw the little guy being walked on and taken advantage of. I feel he would have been proud of me for having written this book.

CONTENTS

Introduction

I first thought of writing this book one evening while driving home somewhat dejected. I had been working with a "For Sale By Owner," trying to convince him to list his property with the real estate firm for which I worked, and lo and behold he'd turned around and sold it himself. In parting, he thanked me and said he could never have done it without my invaluable help.

As I walked to my car, I decided to reassess the approach I had been using with the For Sale By Owners. Too many sold on their own. Too many said, "Thank you for your invaluable help." I was doing something seriously wrong.

I worked on the principle that after I had given the seller some assistance, he, by the law of averages, would be unable to sell his own home because he lacked the total marketing program offered by our firm. I performed numerous helpful services for all of the By Owners I was trying to list: left "Open House" signs; wrote newspaper ads; offered timely mortgage information; did "free, no obligation" market appraisals of residences; explained how to qualify the buyers and, more importantly, why; gave them "free" literature on how to show their homes to prospective buyers; and explained VA, FHA, points, etc. I even offered to come over and fill in the contracts when they found buyers.

It was a surefire system that continually backfired. I was giving them too much help! Then I wondered, what if I gave all of the For Sale By Owners across the country too much help? What if I listed, step by step, how to properly sell a home By Owner in terms that could be easily understood by the general public? What if I supplied them with all the signs and forms necessary to properly market a home? On that evening this book was born.

I seriously feel that the system of merchandising real estate that is thoroughly explained in this book will completely change the complexion of the general residential real estate market as we know it today. Real estate brokerage has undergone little basic change since it first came into being in the early 1700s. Since then, the only real innovation has been the formation and wide usage of the "Multiple Listing Services." Qualifications for becoming a real estate salesman were low in the 1700s, and they are still low today. The state in which I have my real estate license just increased its requirements for licensure. It is now necessary in Illinois for applicants to have completed 30 hours of training prior to the written examination. That's the same amount of time my daughter spends in grammar school in one week. I can unequivocally state that you can learn more from this book than the average real estate salesperson knows after having been licensed by the state. And most likely he's the one knocking at your door right now, trying to get his first listing.

The local and national real estate associations constantly advertise how "professional" they are! This type of advertising wouldn't be necessary if it were true. When was the last time your lawyer or doctor advertised that he was professional? If a lawyer had spent only five days studying law, you wouldn't want him to represent you in a court of law even if the purported offense were a mere parking violation.

It is my opinion that the residential real estate salesman is an anachornism in this day and age. He serves no real purpose other than to chauffeur people around who could just as well chauffeur themselves around and to look for sellers who really don't want to be found by a broker. These two facets of his work involve 95 per cent of his day, and in actuality they are total wastes of time. They are also the reason why brokerage fees are so exorbitantly high in relation to the service rendered.

The picture of inefficiency and low productivity that emerges from the vast majority of real estate offices tends to prove that their necessity is questionable in the least. The functions they perform can be accomplished more satisfactorily by lawyers, appraisers and bankers; and it goes without saying that the savings to the seller alone make For Sale By Owner the only rational way to market a residence.

I sincerely feel that the public interests will be better served when the appreciable costs of brokers' commissions are eliminated from the selling prices of all homes.

This book will cover 99 per cent of the questions and problems you will have in the sale of your home, and your real estate lawyer will be able to answer any other unusual questions that may arise. But if you have any specific problems you would like to discuss, please feel free to write directly to me in care of the publisher (he'll forward it immediately to my Swiss mailbox).

As of this writing, I am still employed by a broker. When this book is published I realize I'll lose a lot of friends, and this fact troubles me deeply. Practically every night I have a tortured nightmare in which hordes of unemployed real estate salesmen carry flaming torches up the winding and narrow road leading to the dark and shadowy castle in which I reside on the top of a high, steep mountain. They then cross the moat and malevolently start battering down the front doors with a heavy timber. Crazed and screaming, they rush in and quickly set fire to my vast piles of "Open House" signs, "Home Information Forms," "Home For Sale By Owner" signs, "Confidential Buyer Qualification Forms," "Showing Registers," "Home For Sale By Owner" books, and especially "Real Estate Salesmen Not Welcome" signs. Still crazed and screaming, they slowly run out of the castle, which by now is bright and flaming, and dance hand in hand around the moat, singing with a mad gleam in their eyes, "The king of the By Owners is dead. Long live the Broker!" As the flames savagely encompass my every fiber, my last thought is, "If only someone could tell the By Owners that the brokers are coming! the brokers are coming!"

I hope you find this book informative, interesting and enjoyable. This could have been a dry subject except that I watered it down. But if per chance you fall asleep before the end of this book, I won't take offense. I'll just assume you finished reading before I was able to finish writing.

1

Real Estate Salesmen Not Welcome ! ! !

Let me be the first to congratulate you on your wise decision to sell your home without the assistance of a real estate broker. With the aid of this book, a knowledgeable real estate lawyer, and an experienced local fee appraiser, you'll save approximately $3,000 (the national mean average of the real estate broker's commission on the sale of a single family residence). Most real estate brokers are presently charging 6 per cent to 7 per cent of the selling price of a home, which in most cases is a lot of money for very little service. The real estate commission you are now about to save will go a long way toward furnishing your new home or toward your children's college education. Or even better, use it to take your wife or lover on a trip around the world.

Before we go any further, please realize that as soon as you plant your "For Sale by Owner" sign and put your ad in the newspaper, the brokers are coming! the brokers are coming! They'll be ringing your front and back doorbells and your phone all at the same time. You'll see them from 9:00 in the morning to 11:00 at night. I am sorry to say you'll find the majority quite rude; they'll badger you beyond belief.

Inevitably, some real estate salesman will say that he wishes to move into your neighborhood and is very interested in personally purchasing your home. He then requests a tour of your home so that he can determine if it will suit the needs of his family, and you say, "Come in, come in. Let me show you around." Afterward, the salesman states that he would like to come back in the evening, when both you and your spouse are present, so that the property can be further discussed and negotiated. You become ecstatic. Your home has been up for sale only one day and already you have a strong potential buyer: he just happens to be a real estate salesman with no ulterior motives(?). Later that evening he comes back and advises you and your spouse that he could actually net you more money by marketing your home through normal real estate channels than if he were to buy it himself. This is true(?) because he can't offer as much for your property as you can expect to secure from another buyer. The sales principle he brings into play here is simple. If he can dash your hopes of a quick sale, maybe he can get a quick listing and make a fast buck. This listing technique is very effective and works time and time again.

All you need is a couple of salesmen like the aforementioned gentleman and you'll start to feel they're trying to get 7 per cent of your flesh rather than of your pocketbook. If you're not prepared, you'll find these meetings with real estate salesmen an ordeal by fire. They are fully prepared to do battle to get your listing, whatever the cost; and they know you're delving into an area in which you are most likely green and unwashed.

You'll find that each broker asks practically the same questions. Know the questions and why they are being asked, and you won't be caught off guard.

(1) "May I assist you in the sale of your home?" You should be able to come up with about $3,000 worth of reasons to say no.

(2) "How much are you asking?" If you've priced your home at or below market value, he's going to be very anxious to list your property.

(3) "Have you had any good offers yet?" The purpose of this question is to make you feel deficient and inferior — and in need of a broker. He knows you haven't had any firm offers yet; otherwise your "For Sale" sign would be down.

(4) "How much longer are you going to try to sell your home on your own?" This leading question should always be answered, "Until I succeed!"

(5) "Have you been advertising in the newspapers?" He's assuming you've had poor results. Tell him otherwise.

(6) "May I see the inside of your home?" If you let him in, he feels he is halfway home to a listing.

(7) "Why are you selling?" If you're being transferred, you're classified as a motivated seller: you have to move. The salesman will then become very persistent because he fully realizes your situation. If it really doesn't matter when you sell your home, the salesman will lose interest because you are not a motivated seller and are most likely trying to sell it over market value.

(8) "Where are you moving?" He'll get a 20 per cent referral fee if he can tie you to a broker in some other area.

(9) "Do you know how to fill out a sales contract?" After you read this book you will.

(10) "Would you like a free appraisal of the market value of your home?" Just tell the salesman that you wanted to be positive that your selling price was at market value and therefore hired a professional appraiser. A fee appraiser has no ulterior motive. Hire him to determine what the best possible selling price will be for your home; once he has afforded this service, he's no longer in your employ. To accept a "free appraisal" from a broker is a lot like going to a dentist for a heart transplant — the risk factor tends to be slightly higher.

(11) "Would you like to borrow an "Open House" sign?" No, you already have one.

Always remember that the broker doesn't make any money until a house is sold. What's more, the sooner he sells a house the more profit he earns because his advertising cost will be very low. Assuming a home is marketed properly, the most important factor in determining how soon it will sell is the price. A bargain home can sell in 24 hours, while an overpriced home can take years to attract a buyer. Obviously, a broker prefers to list a bargain home because the net profit is so much higher. Quite often when a broker is "appraising" a home he'll try to find out what is the least amount of money the seller will accept. This type of question would never be asked by a professional appraiser since it has no pertinence to the market value. It is not uncommon for a broker to come up with an "appraised valuation" equal to the minimum a seller will accept for his home.

The other extreme is also probable. When listings are scarce and competition is heavy, a broker will often highball a seller just to get his signature for 90 days. He'll tell the seller that he's confident that through his unique marketing program he'll be able to sell this home for 20 per cent over market value. Of course, this is untrue. A marketing program only informs prospective buyers as to the availability of the house; it can't raise the selling price over market value. In about three or four weeks the broker will come back and say that general market conditions necessitate a "price adjustment" of 20 per cent (it sounds better than a price reduction). At that point he will have a salable piece of real estate and will have beaten out the competition. The only person who loses will be the seller, who could have sold it at that price and saved thousands of commission dollars.

In conclusion, there is practically no way for you to stop the onslaught of telephone calls from brokers other than by actually having your phone disconnected. All you can really do is tell them you don't need their services and hope they'll have the courtesy not to bother you again. You can stop them from harassing you at your front door by putting up a "Real Estate Salesmen Not Welcome!!!" sign. It works like magic! They know that if they solicit a home with such a sign they can be reported to the local police, the state real estate licensing bureau and the local real estate board. Those five little words are guaranteed to give ou and your family peace of mind.

2

Real Estate Project No. 6

The Florida Association of Realtors undertook a project survey to determine the experiences of a large number of sellers with and without the assistance of brokers. The cities of Orlando and Gainesville were selected for the survey because previous experience indicated that the two areas were reasonably representative of most urban regions. These realtors undertook Project No. 6 with the hope that the results of the survey would be promotionally advantageous to the brokers.

The end result was exactly opposite to what they had expected. At one point the report itself states that the conclusions are very discouraging. For the benefit of the real estate brokers, the report should have been burned along with the researchers. Instead, it was banished to the dark corners of a few selected realtor libraries across the country. Normal people are not allowed in these libraries, only realtors. They must have assumed that no one would ever find out what had transpired. The book is appropriately bound in black.

Project No. 6 consisted of questionnaire mailed to a cross-section of sellers who had used brokers and sellers who had not. The most noteworthy conclusions of the survey are as follows:

Q: Was the closing satisfactory?

Of sellers who sold through a broker, 72.5% said yes, while 95% of sellers who sold By Owner said yes to the same question. This response tends to show that instead of making the transaction smooth, the broker acts as a hinderance. One of the principal reasons for dissatisfaction at broker-handled closings was the failure of the broker to inform the seller of what the costs would be. The sellers also complained that at the closing the broker was more on the buyer's side: he seemed to forget who was paying his commission.

The 5% of By Owner sellers who ran into trouble at the closing felt it was due to mistakes on the part of their attorney.

Be sure your real estate attorney is well versed in local property transactions. Don't be part of the 5%!

Q: Did your broker earn his commission? (to the sellers who sold through brokers)

Fewer than 47% of the sellers in Gainesville said yes. This is very surprising because most people do not want to admit that they've wasted their money. It's human nature for a person to try to conceal his mistakes.

Q: Would you ever use a real estate broker again?

Fewer than 39% of the sellers in Gainesville said yes. The report stated that this was far from being a happy situation — an understatement to say the least.

Q: Why are you selling your home without a broker? (to By Owners)

Seventy-one per cent felt that commissions were too high and unearned; 16.5% had sold their last homes without any difficulties and felt they didn't need a broker; 12.5% had had bad experiences with a broker previously.

Q: Did you have any problems in selling your home without a broker?

Seventy-five per cent of By Owner sellers had no problems in finding a buyer and bringing the transaction to fruition with the assistance of a lawyer.

Q: Did you have any problems in the sale of your home that a broker could have solved?

Of By Owner sellers, 97% stated that there were no problems in the course of the real estate transaction that a broker might have been of assistance in solving. There were no problems in the recording of the deed, bringing title down, escrow and similar matters. Many of those who had previously used brokers stated that they were pleased to learn they could do it themselves as long as they had a good real estate attorney.

It has always been assumed that a home will sell faster if it is sold through a real estate broker. The survey proved this to be untrue. In both cities the figures showed that the By Owner seller of a lower priced home sold his residence faster than a broker marketing a like property. Higher priced homes sold slightly faster through brokers, but in this instance the time span on any individual transaction could favor either group.

Finally, the survey also uncovered the fact that there is a prevalent belief on the part of most buyers that a home being marketed through a broker is priced higher, by the amount of commission, than a By Owner property. These buyers feel the broker just tacks his commission onto the fair market price of the home. Rather than paying these inflated prices, the buyer would much rather deal directly with the seller. This is one of the main reasons the By Owner didn't have a problem in selling their home.

3

Get a Real Estate Lawyer

When you're selling your home on your own, the most important person in the world is your lawyer. If he's incompetent, he'll gum up the works beyond belief. If he's proficient, everything will run as smoothly as the movement in a Swiss watch. If the lawyer you are presently using is a general practitioner, do not use him for your real estate transactions. Please read the following sentence 100 times:

■ *Real estate transactions should be handled only by full-time real estate lawyers.*

In order for the sale of your home to be trouble free, it is of the utmost importance that your lawyer be highly knowledgeable in local real estate transactions. If he deals in all facets of law, his actual know-how in each individual area will be quite limited, and this obviously will be to your detriment. In addition, if he has a trial coming up, the last thing he's going to worry about is the closing of the sale of your home. You are going to need frequent advice about the contract, escrow, contingencies, etc., and if he's not there to solve these problems,

you're going to be completely lost, without anyone to turn to.

If you don't have a good real estate lawyer in mind, do not call your local bar association for advice. They automatically lump the good with the bad and won't tell you the difference. All you have to do is call your local bank or savings and loan association; they will be happy to recommend several reputable attorneys who specialize in real estate. Whatever you do, don't pick one out of a hat.

Your attorney's job is to protect your rights, advise you to the best of his ability, and handle all the legal instruments necessary to facilitate the sale of your home.

Don't be afraid to discuss the attorney's fee with him beforehand. A normal By Owner residential real estate transaction usually costs the seller between $200 and $250 in attorney fees. These are monies well spent. You will have the satisfaction of knowing that your rights and best interests have been represented fully.

4

Your Home Will Sell if the Price is Right ! ! !

A realistic selling price is perhaps the most important consideration to the buyer of your home. Supply and demand affect the price of real estate much the same as they do other items in the marketplace. Therefore, arriving at the right price on your home is of utmost importance.

Overpricing accomplishes nothing, and the overpriced home will not be in competition with similar homes currently for sale on the market. Nearly 100 per cent of all homes sell at their fair market value. The question is, how does one arrive at the fair market value?

Considerable skill and judgment are needed to appraise property with accuracy. Appraising is not an exact science and therefore requires continual education on all phases of the real estate business. The best person to contact is a local fee appraiser. Your real estate lawyer will be happy to recommend one. The better appraisers belong to such national appraisal groups as Member of the Appraisers Institute (MAI) or Society of Real Estate Appraisers (SREA). The average charge is less than $100. The complete procedure includes obtaining all the physical information: room dimensions, lot size, taxes, assessments, type and quality of construction, exterior dimensions, distances to schools, shopping, churches, transportation, age of the property, inclusions, amenities, obsolescence, etc.

Since the marketability of the property is the basic test value, your appraiser will pick out comparable homes in the general area of the property that have recently sold. The sale price of these homes is then adjusted plus or minus in comparison to what your home does or doesn't have.

Most of us know someone who has priced his home well over market value and after waiting and waiting sold it some two years later. This seller feels that it is just a matter of waiting for the right buyer to come along, but this is untrue. What really happens is that during the two years, the general used-home market in the area appreciates to such an extent that the home is at market value when it finally sells.

Actually, it's easy to determine when an

overpriced home will sell. Let's assume that it's priced 30% over market value. If the general used-home market is appreciating at 10% per year, it will take three years before Mr. Right Buyer knocks on the seller's overpriced door.

Now it's up to you. If you agree that homes priced too high are extremely difficult to sell and that your home must compete with comparable homes on the market, you must price it right. National statistics show that a home priced within 5% of fair market value is 10 times more likely to sell than a home priced at 15% to 20% over market value.

The following is a list of 65 items and amenities and what their probable value is. Please understand, it is to be used only as a guide. The dollar values are an average and will vary from one area or one house to the next. You should find it very handy and informative, and it will give you a good rule of thumb to roughly determine the value of your home in comparison to other homes presently on the market.

THE APPROXIMATE DOLLAR AMOUNT
A POTENTIAL BUYER WILL PAY FOR THE FOLLOWING ITEMS

Aluminum siding . . . $1,000
Attic exhaust fan . . . $ 50
Awnings . . . no value
Basement (full $3,000, ½ $2,000, partial $1,500) . . . $1,000 to $3,000
Bath (full $1,000, ½ $500) . . . $ 500 to $1,000
Bedrooms (additional) . . . $2,200
Blacktop driveway . . . $ 500
Brick construction . . . $ 150 to $300

Built-in bar ($150, wet $300)	$ 150 to $300
Built-in bookcases	no value
Built-in oven and range	$ 175
Built-in stero system	$ 200
Carpeting lr $300 — dr $200 — kit $100 — fr $200 — br $200	$ 100 to $300/room
Central air conditioning	$1,000
Central vacuum system	$ 300
Ceramic entry $150 — quarry tile $250	$ 150 to $250
Concrete driveway	$ 600
Condition	$1,000 to $2,500
Combination storm and screens	$ 400
Curtains	no value to $150
Dishwasher portable — $75 built-in — $175	$ 75 to $175
Disposal	$ 40
Drapes lr $200 — dr $150 — other $75	$ 75 to $200
Dryer (clothes)	$ 75
Electric garage door opener	$ 110
Electronic air filter	$ 125
Family room addition	$3,250
Fireplace: brick $1,100 — stone $1,300 — electric $50	$ 150 to $1,300
Fireplace equipment	$ 35
First-floor utility or laundry room	$ 400
Florida room	$1,000
Freezer	$ 125
Gas barbecue $75 — brick $150	$ 75 to $150
Gas pole lights $25 — electric no value	no value to $25
Garage: 1 car $1,200 — 2 car $2,100	$1,200 to $2,100
Gutters and downspouts	$ 225
Heated garage	$ 90
Humidifier	$ 50
Intercom system	$ 75
Landscaping	$1,000
Location	$1,000 to $3,000
Patio: open $350 — covered $650	$ 350 to $650

Playhouse/swing set	no value
Pool: in ground $3,000 — above ground $450	$ 450 to $3,000
Pool table	$ 125
Recreation room	$1,500
Refrigerator	$ 125
Riding lawn mower	$ 150
Slab — (deduct)	$(-500)
Screened-in porch	$ 600
Snow blower	$ 100
Storage shed (wood or steel)	$ 100
Stove	$ 125
Rotor TV antenna	$ 50
Trash compactor	$ 65
Washer	$ 90
Water softener	$ 165
Wax-free floor	$ 100
Window air conditioner	$ 65

There are a multitude of factors that come into play in determining the true market value of a single-family residence. The accompanying list emphasizes the more important of these positive and negative elements.

(1) *The number of homes for sale within a ½-mile radius.* If there are many homes for sale within a specified area, then the market value or selling price will be lower for all the homes because the supply is greater than the demand.

(2) *The affect of new-home and apartment construction on the used-home market.* Normally, the prices of used homes follow the rising prices for new homes.

Every time you hear that the carpenters or electricians get a 10 per cent increase, you know that these are added costs to the contractor and will be directly reflected in the selling prices of these homes. Most people, however, do not realize that these increases are directly reflected in selling prices of used homes. The reason is simple: new homes and used homes are in direct competition with each other.

(3) *The market trend of the real estate values in your area.* Is the local population increasing (property values will go up) or decreasing (property values will go down)?

(4) *Unfavorable property characteristics.* These include location on a busy street, red carpeting, poor floor plan, poor location, overimprovement, community driveway (easement), poor landscaping, no garage, inadequate eating space, minimal closet space, small kitchen-counter and cabinet space, one or two bedrooms, only one bath, single-car garage, below-average demand for this style home, below-average demand for the area the home is located in, built prior to 1925, or poor quality of construction.

(5) *Favorable property characteristics.* On a clear day you can see forever; beautiful landscaping, swimming pool, family room, two or more baths, four or more bedrooms, party room, den, close to "everything," secluded setting, community recreation facilities, fabulous floor plan, exterior maintained to perfection, top-notch school district, quality construction, heavy demand for this style home, heavy demand for this area, three car garage, quality carpeting and drapes (included in price), or special seller-provided financing.

■ The following is an example of a form that many residential appraisers use when they make an analysis of the sellers property.

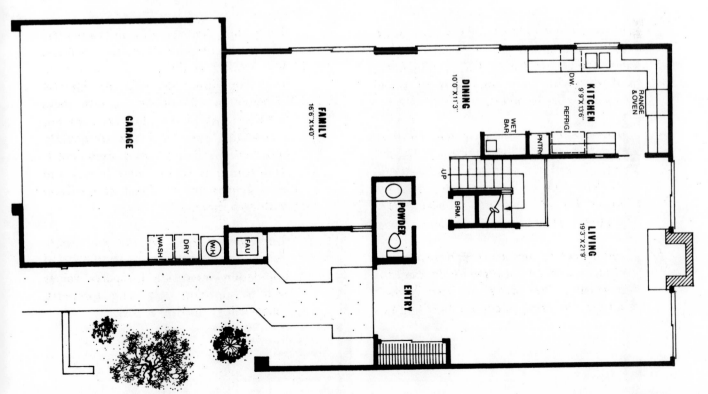

RESIDENTIAL APPRAISAL REPORT

File No. _____

To be completed by Lender

Borrower/Client **Gerald M. & Sandra J. Steiner**   Census Tract **A14**   Map Reference **49C7**

Property Address **92 Watergate**

City **South Barrington**   County **Cook**   State **Ca.**   Zip Code **11010**

Legal Description **Lot #92 in the Coves of S. Barrington Unit Three, being a Subdivision in Sections 26 & 27, Township 42 N., Range 9, East of the Third Principal Meridian**

Current Sale Price (if applicable) $ **148,500.**   Date of Sale ____   Property Rights Appraised ☒ Fee ☐ Leasehold ☐ Condo ☐ PUD

Actual Real Estate Taxes $ **1,871.57 1974** (yr) Special Assessments $ **200.00** Payable $ **200.00** per yr. for **–** yrs.; or, ☐ to be paid in full at settlement

Lender **1st Federal S.&L. Assoc.**   Lender's Address **1 S. Dearborn St.**

Appraiser **John R. Mc Mahon**   Directions or Instructions to Appraiser: **Barrington Rd. to Mundhank Rd., West to Witt, North to Watergate, West to address.**

NEIGHBORHOOD

Location — Urban ☐ Suburban ☐ Rural ☒

Built Up — Over 75% ☐ 25% to 75% ☐ Under 25% ☒

Growth Rate ☐ Fully Dev. Rapid ☐ Steady ☒ Slow ☐

Property Values — Increasing ☒ Stable ☐ Weak ☐ Declining ☐

Demand/Supply — In Balance ☒ Shortage ☐ Over Supply ☐

Marketing Time — Under 3 Mos. ☐ 4–6 Mos. ☒ Over 6 Mos. ☐

Present Use **100**% 1 Family ____% 2–4 Family ____% Apts. ____% ____

Change in Use — Not Likely ☒ Likely ☐ Taking Place ☐

Predominant Occupancy — Owner ☒ Tenant ☐ ____% Vacant

Price Range $ **100M** to $ **300M** Predominant Value $ **130M**

Age **0** yrs to **5** yrs Predominant Age **2** yrs

	Good	Avg.	Fair	Poor
Employment Stability	☒	☐	☐	☐
Adequacy of Shopping	☐	☐	☒	☐
Convenience to Schools	☐	☐	☒	☐
Quality of Schools	☐	☒	☐	☐
Recreational Facilities	☐	☒	☐	☐
Level of Taxes	☐	☐	☒	☐
Adequacy of Utilities	☒	☐	☐	☐
Neighborhood Compatibility	☒	☐	☐	☐
Protection from Adverse Influence	☒	☐	☐	☐
Police and Fire Protection	☐	☒	☐	☐
General Appearance of Properties	☒	☐	☐	☐
Appeal to Market	☒	☐	☐	☐

Comments: **Home is located in the center of the subdivision ... general changes in peripheral zoning will not tend to devalue this site.**

SITE

Dimensions **150'** x **360.7** x ____ x ____ = **55,995** Sq. Ft. **1.285 A** ☐ Corner Lot

Zoning **Residential**   Highest and Best Use: ☒ Present Use ☐ Other ____

	Public	Comm.	Individual
Elec.	☒	☐	☐
Gas	☒	☐	☐
Water	☐	☐	☒
Sanitary Sewer	☐	☐	Septic Tank ☒

Cess Pool ☐

Street ☒ Public ☐ Private
Surface **Asphalt**
☐ Storm Sewer
☐ Curb and Gutter
☐ Sidewalk
☐ Street Lights
☐ Alley

☒ Underground Utilities
☐ Fences (type) **against zoning**
☒ Driveway (surface) **crushed stone**

	Good	Avg.	Fair	Poor
Topography	☒	☐	☐	☐
Size & Shape of Lot	☒	☐	☐	☐
Drainage	☒	☐	☐	☐

View Amenity **scenic view of lake**
Easements **utilities and covenants**
Encroachments **none**
Flood Conditions **on flood plane / 8' above lake**
Adverse Influences **none**
Comments: **One of the most prime sites in the subdivision.**

IMPROVEMENTS

☒ Existing (approx. yr. blt.) 19**73**
☐ Proposed Construction
☐ Under Construction

☒ Detached ☐ Semi-detached ☐ Row
Dwelling Units **1**   Stories **2**

Design (Rambler, Split Level, etc.) **2 story / Spanish**   Exterior Walls **brick & frame**

Roof **Shingle**   Gutters & Downspouts ☐ None **Sheet Metal**   Windows (Type) ☐ Storm Sash ☒ Screens **Thermopane** ☐ Combination   Insulation ☒ Ceiling ☒ Roof ☒ Walls

Foundation Walls **Cement**   ☒ Crawl Space   ☐ Slab on Grade

BSMT. **85** % Basement ☐ Outside Entrance ☒ Concrete Floor ☒ Floor Drain ☒ Sump Pump   Evidence of: ☐ Dampness ☐ Termites ☐ Settlement

Finished Ceiling **Partial**   Finished Walls **Partial**   Finished Floor **Partial**

Comments: **Finished movie theater located in basement.**

ROOM LIST

	BASEMENT LEVEL	FIRST LEVEL	SECOND LEVEL	THIRD LEVEL
Entry	☐	☒	☐	☐
Living Room	☐	☒	☐	☐
Dining Room	☐	☒	☐	☐
Dining Alcove	☐	☐	☐	☐
Kitchen	☐	☒	☐	☐
No. of Bedrooms			4	
Family Room	☐	☒	☐	☐
Theater	☒	☐	☐	☐
Den	☐	☒	☐	☐
Full Bath(s)		1	2	
3/4 Bath(s)				
Half Bath(s)				

INTERIOR FINISH

Floors: ☐ Hardwood ☒ Carpet Over **Plywood** ____
Walls: ☒ Drywall ☐ Plaster
Trim & Finish ☒ Good ☐ Average ☐ Fair ☐ Poor
Bath Floor: ☒ Ceramic ☐ Composition ☐ ____
Bath Wainscote ☒ Ceramic ☐ ____
Special Features: **1** Fireplaces (List Other) **Beamed cathedral ceiling in family room.**
ATTIC: ☒ Yes ☐ No ☐ Stairway ☐ Drop-stair ☐ Floored ☐ Heated   ☐ Finished (Describe)

CAR STORAGE: Garage ☐ Built-in ☒ Attached ☐ Detached ☐ Car Port
No. Cars **2½** ☒ Adequate ☐ Inadequate   Condition **excellant**
PORCHES, PATIOS, POOL, etc. (describe) **Patios 17'X50' & 10'X34', Courtyard 17'3"X21, Balcony 4'X14'**

EQUIPMENT

Kitchen
☒ Range/Oven
☒ Dishwasher
☒ Fan/Hood
☒ Disposal
☒ Refrigerator
☒ Washer
☒ Dryer

CABINETS
☒ Adequate
☐ Inadequate

Heat: Type **Forced air**
Fuel: ☒ Gas ☐ Elec ☐ Oil ☐ Coal
A.C.: ☐ Central ☐ Other ____
☐ Adequate ☐ Inadequate
☒ Washer ☒ Dryer
Other Equipment (List) **Burglar alarm & fire alarm**

OVERALL PROPERTY RATING

	Good	Avg.	Fair	Poor
Quality of Construction (Materials & Finish)	☒	☐	☐	☐
Condition of Improvements	☒	☐	☐	☐
Rooms size and layout	☒	☐	☐	☐
Closets and Storage	☒	☐	☐	☐
Plumbing—adequacy and condition	☒	☐	☐	☐
Electrical—adequacy and condition	☒	☐	☐	☐
Compatibility to Neighborhood	☒	☐	☐	☐
Overall Livability	☒	☐	☐	☐
Appeal and Marketability	☒	☐	☐	☐

Effective Age **50** Yrs. Estimated Remaining Economic Life **47** Yrs.

COMMENTS (Special features, functional or physical inadequacies, repairs needed, modernization, etc.)
Residence is in 'like new' condition and tastefully decorated.

ATTACH DESCRIPTIVE PHOTOGRAPHS OF SUBJECT PROPERTY AND STREET SCENE

PURPOSE OF APPRAISAL: To estimate Market Value.

DEFINITION OF MARKET VALUE: The highest price which the property will bring contemplating the consummation of a sale and the passing of full title from seller to buyer by deed, under conditions whereby: buyer and seller are free of undue stimulus and are motivated by no more than the reactions of typical participants; both parties are well-informed or well-advised and act prudently, each for what he considers his own best interest; a reasonable exposure is given in the open market; and payment is made in cash or on terms reasonably equivalent to cash assuming typical financing terms available in the community for similar property.

COST APPROACH

EXTERIOR BUILDING SKETCH (Optional)

Measurements		No. Stories		Sq. Ft.
28.1 x 50.1	x	2	=	2,815.6
16.1 x 21.5	x	1	=	346.2
31.4 x 13	x	1	=	408.2
x		x		

Total Gross Living Area (List in (1) below) . . . 3,570.

ESTIMATED LAND VALUE (If leasehold, show only leasehold value)		$ 34,695.00

ESTIMATED REPRODUCTION COST—NEW—OF IMPROVEMENTS:
Site Improvements (driveway, landscaping, etc.)

Driveway & landscaping		2,200.00
Dwelling 3,570 Sq. Ft. @ 26.60	=	94,962.00
999.8 Sq. Ft. @ 3.70	=	3,699.26
Extras Beach 150' X 3.50	=	525.00
Well & septic	=	6,800.00
Porches, Patio, etc. 17'X22' + 17'X50' + 10'X34'	=	2,450.00
Garage/Car Port 515 Sq. Ft. @ 15.30	=	7,879.00
Total Estimated Cost New	=	118,515.76
Less Depreciation Physical $ 4% Functional $ .00 Economic $ .00	(−) $	4,748.25
Depreciated value of improvements		113,727.51

INDICATED VALUE BY COST APPROACH $148,422.51

Land Sales (Recite Sales and Compare to Subject if appropriate for this appraisal) Lot #112, 1.6 acre sold for $43,200.00
Lot #151, .9 acre sold for $24,300.00   Lot #128, 1.2 acre sold for $32,400.00

MARKET DATA ANALYSIS

The market data selected are the most recent sales of properties, similar and proximate to subject, known to the undersigned, that a buyer of subject property would have given consideration to purchasing. In the absence of actual sales an explanation is included in the comments section below. The following analysis, of the recited sales, sets forth a description and a dollar adjustment, of the estimated amount which the local market would recognize for the items of significant variation between subject property and the comparative sale.

If an item in comparable property is superior to, or more favorable than, the subject property, a minus (-) adjustment is made, thus reducing the indicated value of subject; if a significant item in comparable is inferior to, or less favorable than, the subject property, a plus (+) adjustment is made, thus increasing the indicated value of the subject.

LIST ONLY THOSE ITEMS THAT REQUIRE ADJUSTMENT.

ITEM	Subject Property	COMPARABLE NO. 1		COMPARABLE NO. 2		COMPARABLE NO. 3	
Address	92 Watergate S.Barrington	114 Back Bay Rd. S.Barrington		159 Upper Pond Rd. S.Barrington		131 Turning Shore S.Barrington	
Proximity to Subj.		1 block		2 blocks		½ block	
	DESCRIPTION	DESCRIPTION	+ (−) $ Adjustment	DESCRIPTION	+ (−) $ Adjustment	DESCRIPTION	+ (−) $ Adjustment
Sale date (Time adj.)	−	8/12/75	+1,500.	7/22/75	+2,000.	11/1/75	+450.
Site and Location	1.285 acres riparian	.825 acre non-riparian	+19,850.	1.1 acres non-riparian	+14,900.	.73 acre riparian	+15,000.
Design and Construction	Spanish brick/frame	Colonial brick/frame	−	Tudor frame	+500.	Colonial brick	−500.
Age and Condition	3 years excellant	5 years excellant	+3,800.	0 years excellant	−5,700.	2 years excellant	−1,900.
Room Count & Livable Area(1)	Total 11 / B-rms 4 / Baths 3 — 3,570 Sq.Ft.	Total 9 / B-rms 4 / Baths 2½ — 3,210 Sq.Ft.	+6,625	Total 10 / B-rms 4 / Baths 2½ — 3,840 Sq.Ft.	−7,180	Total 11 / B-rms 5 / Baths 2½ — 4,220 Sq.Ft.	−17,290
Functional Util.	excellant	excellant	−	excellant	−	excellant	−
Basement & Bsmt finished rooms	partially fin. bsmt.	bsmt. not finished	+9,340	bsmt. not finished	+9,340	bsmt. not finished	+9,340
Garage/Car Port	2½ car	3½ car	−2,600	2½ car	−	2½ car	−
Porches, Patio Pool, etc.	2 patios 1 courtyard	1 patio 1 pool	−4,550	1 patio	+1,650	1 patio 1 pool	−4,550
Air Conditioning	no	yes	−1,500	yes	−1,500	yes	−1,500
Financing	−						
Sales Price	148,500.00	115,000.		136,000.		159,000.	
Net Adj. +(−)		+32,465.		+14,010.		−9,500.	
Indicated Value of Subject		147,465.		150,010.		149,500.	

INDICATED VALUE BY MARKET DATA APPROACH . . . . $ 148,500.

INDICATED VALUE BY INCOME APPROACH (If applicable). Fair Market Rent $ _ /Mo. x Gross Rent Multiplier _ = $ _

This appraisal is made subject to the repairs, alterations, or conditions listed below; or, ☐ Completion per plans and specifications.

Correlation & Comments: not applicable.

I certify, that to the best of my knowledge and belief. the statements made in this report are true and I have not knowingly withheld any significant information; that I have personally inspected subject property, both inside and out; that I have no interest, present or contemplated, in subject property or the participants in the sale; that neither the employment nor compensation to make said appraisal is contingent upon my value estimate; and, that all contingent and limiting conditions are stated herein (*). Title is assumed to be good and marketable.

I ESTIMATE THE MARKET VALUE, AS DEFINED, OF SUBJECT PROPERTY AS OF 12/1 19 75 to be $ 148,500.00

* ☐ (FHLMC Form 439) Certification and Statement of Limiting Conditions Applies ☒ On file with client ☐ Attached.

Signed: *John R. McMahon* Appraiser(s)

FHLMC 70 Rev 5 —Reverse

5

Repainting and Repairing Always Repays

One of the most important steps in the process of selling your home for the best possible price in the least amount of time is to carefully and properly prepare it for inspection by potential buyers. This step is equally important whether you sell it on your own or list your home with a real estate broker.

Yes, it's true that a house will eventually sell no matter what condition it's in, but the condition is always disproportionately reflected in the sales price. If your home needs $1,000 in repair work, you'll have to drop your selling price by at least $3,000 unless you decide to invest the money to remedy the condition. The reason for this is obvious when you think about it. The only type of person looking for a home in need of repairs is a "bargain hunter." He will never pay top dollar, and he'll come in with a low-ball bid and most likely not budge one red cent. The bargain hunter is traditionally the worst potential buyer to deal with. Inevitably, he'll try to beat you into the ground and kick sand in your face. Your life will be that much brighter if a bargain hunter never darkens your door. Before you put your home on the market, be sure to make all needed repairs!!! Try to make your home the showplace of the block.

Quite often the seller is not a good judge of what painting and repairs should be done. He has lived in the house for some years and has learned to overlook certain things that a prospective buyer might feel are serious drawbacks. If at all possible, have a disinterested third party, such as the appraiser, go through your home and make suggestions on anything that will tend to increase the sale price. Take his advice! Don't look on some of his recommendations as being petty: it's the small things that turn an ordinary house into a showplace.

The appearance of the outside of your residence is far more important than you may realize. If a potential buyer doesn't like the exterior, most likely he won't even stop to see the interior. Remember, you can't rely on the inside alone to sell your home because the prospect may never see it. Look at the outside of the house with a very critical eye.

First impressions are lasting impressions. There are a multitude of things you can do to speed the sale of your house. If needed, paint the fence, trellis and garden gate. Mow the lawn every five days, cultivate the flower beds, prune the bushes, give your residence that well-cared-for look.

Loose door knobs, sticking drawers, warped cabinet doors, and other minor items are noticed by the prospective buyer and detract from the value of your home. Be sure to have them fixed. Repair that leaking faucet. The dripping water will discolor the sink and call attention to the possibility that the plumbing is faulty. Repairing all of these will make a big difference.

Faded, dirty walls and worn woodwork reduce the appeal of your home. Don't try to tell a buyer how your home could look. Show him by redecorating first. The results will be a quicker sale at a higter price.

If you give it a through cleaning from top to bottom, you will greatly enhance a prospect's desire to purchase your home. Women are particularly sensitive about bathrooms. Keep them clean and orderly. Be sure they sparkle. Also check and repair the caulking around the bathtubs and showers.

Always let the sun shine in. A dark room will give a prospect the feeling that he's in a funeral parlor. Open the drapes and curtains, turn on the lights if it's a cloudy day, let the prospect see how cheerful your home can be. And in the evening, a brightly lighted house is like a welcome sign. You can turn on a prospect by turning on all of your lights. Be sure to replace any burned out bulbs in the light fixtures.

Bedrooms are always of prime interest to a prospect. Make sure the beds are made and the rooms are kept uncluttered. Attractive bedspreads are always a plus.

Make sure that you don't lose a prospect down a flight of stairs. Keep stairways clear and thereby avoid a cluttered appearance and possible injuries.

Remember the kitchen is the heart of the home, so keep it spotless. No dirty dishes! A well-decorated kitchen speaks great appeal to a prospective "lady of the house." An investment in new kitchen wallpaper will be returned many times over. Don't forget to scrub the range top, exhaust hood, and, most important, the inside of the oven.

Clear out clutter in the closets, basement and garage. Have these areas present as neat an appearance as possible. Discard any old tools, boxes, equipment, or odds and ends that are no longer being used. Now is the time for a garage sale!

A prospective buyer always shudders at the thought of going down into the basement. He knows that if a home has any monsters they'll undoubtedly be lurking in the dark, damp corners of a musty, spider-and-bug-infested basement. In order to dispel these relentless latent fears, paint the walls a light color. This also gets rid of those wavy lines that run horizontally across the walls about four feet above the floor. Which reminds me of the time I

was showing a home that had a slightly dampish basement. After sloshing around for a few minutes, we all decided to go back upstairs because none of us had any scuba gear. I naively asked the seller if there was a condensation problem. He said "no!" He insisted he just hosed down his basement and hadn't had a chance to mop it up yet.

If there's any dampness in your basement, eliminate the cause. A bone-dry basement is a necessity when most potential buyers try to picture it as a recreation room. A dehumidifier is great for eliminating musty odors. Also, while you're down there take a look at your furnace and water heater. If they're old and rusty, give them a thorough cleaning and then a coat of aluminum paint.

Once your home is ready for the "white-glove" test, it's well on the road to being sold.

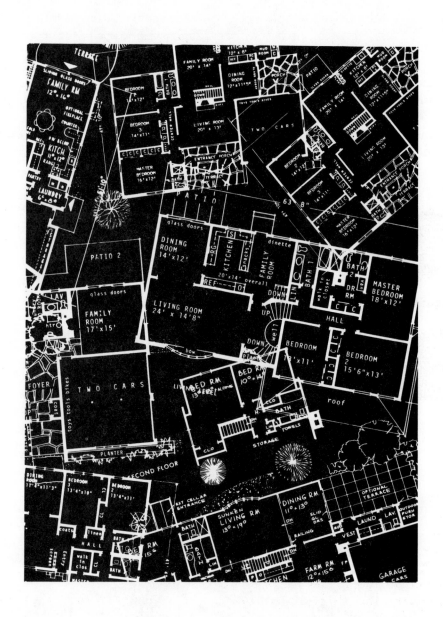

6

Home Information Form

The "Home Information Form," which you will find in the back of this book, is a complete summary description for your property. (The form is perforated for easy removal.) Whether you sell By Owner or through a broker, it will be necessary for you to supply this information. When used properly, the "Home Information Form" is an extremely effective sales tool. It enables you to convey all of the important factual data about your house to a very large number of potential purchasers.

To get the greatest use out of the "Home Information Form," hand it out to every prospective buyer who visits your home. He can then take the form home and use it to compare your house with others he has inspected. The "Home Information Form" will also serve as a constant reminder to the prospective buyer who may have inspected your property weeks ago.

If you receive a telephone inquiry about your home and the prospect is not interested enough to come over, ask him for his name and address so you can mail a "Home Information Form" to him. Explain that it includes all the general information about your residence — *e.g.*, room sizes, taxes, etc. — plus photographs, which describe the property better than words ever can. Always remember that a prospective buyer's motivations and needs can change overnight. Maybe your home isn't suitable for him today: tomorrow it may be perfect.

If you use these forms as often as possible, they by themselves can find the buyer for your home! Give a dozen or two to your wife and ask her to post one in every supermarket she shops at. Don't forget your neighbors! Your good friends will consider it an honor to try to assist you in finding a buyer. If you are enemies with some of your neighbors, give them extra sheets. They'll work hardest of all just to get you moved out as soon as possible.

Please check the order form in the back of this book for the prices for having the "Home Information Form" laid out, typed and printed. (The order form is perforated for easy removal.) Allow a minimum of two weeks for delivery.

Please compile all of the information with due care. Remember, a prospective buyer will rely on this form as fact. A misrepresentation can have legal ramifications. Fill in the form in pencil so you can make changes as necessary after you recheck it. After we print your "Home Information Forms," please go over them, checking for inaccuracies. If we have made a mistake, we'll reprint your order at no charge. To fill out the "Home Information Form" for your residence, just supply the required information and be sure to include two clear black and white photos, 2¼"x3½" (the same size as a "2R" in 35MM). The pictures are acceptable if they can be cut to this size.

■ The "Home Information Form" should be filled out as follows:

(1) *Address.* List your complete address, including the city, state and zip code.

(2) *Faces.* List whether your home faces the north, south, east or west.

(3) *Rooms.* What is the total number of rooms in your home? Exclude bathrooms, utility rooms, workshops and any room that is still unfinished.

(4) *Bedrooms.* List the number of bedrooms.

(5) *Baths.* List the number of bathrooms. If a bathroom doesn't have a shower or tub, it's classified as a ½ bath.

(6) *Price.* List your asking price.

(7) *Owners.* List the complete name of the owners. If the property is in a trust, include the name of the bank, the trust number, the trustee and his phone number.

(8) *Type/Style.* List whether your home is a ranch, split level, two story, Cape Cod, colonial, contemporary, etc.

(9) *Construction.* List whether your

residence is brick, frame or block.

(10) *Lot Size.* Check the survey for this information.

(11) *Lot Description.* Is your land hilly, well landscaped or located on water? Are there a lot of trees and shrubs?

(12) *Possession.* While you can put down 30, 60 or 90 days or even a specific date, if possible, it is always best to write "immediate." Making your home available to a prospective buyer when he finds it most convenient to move is just one more way of creating that extra interest. It may be all a buyer needs to switch from undecided to decisive. And in reality you're the one who determines exactly what immediate is. By the time title is brought down and the mortgage is cleared, most likely the earliest actual possession will be in 30 or 60 days. Listing a specific date is usually not advisable. Assuming the date is May 24, on May 25 a prospective buyer is going to wonder why no one bought your home previously. He'll think something is wrong.

(13) *Age/Builder.* List the age of the house and the name of the builder.

(14) *Purchase Year.* List when you bought the home.

(15) *Schools Par.* If there is a local parochial school, list it here.

(16) *Schools Pub.: Elementary, Junior High, High School.* List the appropriate public schools.

(17) *Condition.* If your home is only in fair condition, make all needed improvements so that you can at least describe it as being in good condition.

(18) *Electric.* List whether you have 100-amp or 200-amp service.

(19) *Heat Cost.* List your total heating bill for the year.

(20) *Gas/Oil/Coal.* Mark the appropriate box.

(21) *Roof/Siding.* Do you have a shake, shingle or tar roof? Do you have aluminum siding or is it frame?

(22) *Sewer/Septic.* Mark the appropriate box.

(23) *Water cost/Well.* Do you have city water? If so, what is the cost? Or do you have a well?

(24) *Rooms/Floor: 1st, 2nd, 3rd floor, Basement, Size.* List the floor each room is on and the size of the room.

(25) *Dining Room.* Is it a combination living room dining room with no separate wall? Is it an L-shaped living room dining room? Or is the dining area a completely separate room?

(26) *Baths.* List the number of baths on each

floor and then the total number in the house.

(27) *Blank Space.* This is for sewing room, workshop, maid's room, darkroom, etc.

(28) *Central Air.* How many tons and what is the brand name.

(29) *Carpeting.* What rooms are carpeted?

(30) *Dishwasher.* Yes or no and brand name.

(31) *Disposal.* Yes or no and brand name.

(32) *Drapes.* Are drapes included? Which rooms?

(33) *Fireplace.* Yes or no and material (brick, stone, marble, etc.).

(34) *Garage.* List whether you have a carport or a garage; whether it is attached or detached; whether it is a one-, two- or three-car garage.

(35) *Patio.* List size and material.

(36) *Porch.* List size and material.

(37) *Oven/Range.* Yes or no — Built-in?

(38) *Stove.* Yes or no and brand name.

(39) *Storm/Screens.* Yes or no or if you are missing some, write "as exist."

(40) *Water Softener.* Mark appropriate boxes.

(41) *Blank Spaces.* Do you have a swimming pool, out buildings, burglar alarm system, outhouse, cabana, etc.?

(42) *Basement.* List size and mark appropriate boxes.

(43) *Other Inclusions.* Are there other items of personal property that you wish to include to sweeten the pot?

(44) *Exclusions.* Are you taking your grandmother's chandelier with you? If you don't take it down now, you must list it as an exclusion; otherwise it will automatically be construed as part of the real estate.

(45) *Directions.* Always start with the closest main artery. Never say right or left — always north, south, east or west.

(46) *Mortgagee.* List the bank or savings and loan association where you have your home loan.

(47) *Mortgage Balance.* How much do you still owe on your home?

(48) *PITI (Principle, Interest, Taxes and Insurance).* How much is your monthly payment?

(49) *Rate.* At what interest rate are you paying on the loan?

(50) *Term.* How many years did you take the loan out for?

(51)   *Assumable.* Can the purchaser of your home take over the balance of your loan?

(52)   *If yes — Service Charge.* How much will the bank charge the purchaser to assume your loan? This charge is often expressed in points.

(53)   *Reason for Selling.* Are you being transferred, relocating, need larger home, need smaller home, liquidating an estate, etc.?

(54)   *Remarks.* This is where you can write how wonderful, fantastic and beautiful your home is. Turn to the chapter called "Creative Advertising" for assistance in completing this section.

(55)   *Photos.* We need two sharp black and white photographs of your home, one frontal and one rear or interior. If the photos you send us are blurred or dark or cockeyed, that's the way they're going to look on the forms we ship back to you. If you aren't a camera bug, it will be worthwhile to have these pictures taken professionally. The finished size must be 2¼"x3½".

■ As soon as you receive these forms, start passing them out. Give one to every prospect. Give two to friends, relatives, neighbors, fellow workers and associates. They will always want to keep one for themselves. Give a couple hundred to your wife.

HOME INFORMATION FORM
This information is believed reliable, but not warranted.

Address	City	State	Zip	Faces	Rooms	Brms.	Baths	Price
92 Watergate,	South Barrington	Ca.	11010	SW	11	4	3	$148,500

Owner(s) Gerald M. + Sandra J. Steiner

Phone (Bus.) (312) 397-7887
Phone (Res.) (312) 381-1745

Type/Style	2 story Spanish
Construction	Brick + Frame
Lot Size	151' X 373' - 1.285 acres
Lot Description	Hilly, 8' above lake
Possession	Immediate
Age/Builder	3 yrs. / M.J. Graft Inc.
Purchase Year	1973
Schools Par.	St. Ann
Schools Pub.	El. Grove Ave.

Jr. Middle School   H.S. Barrington High School

Condition —	Exc. ☒ Good ☐ Fair ☐
Electric —	100 amp ☐ 200 amp ☒
Heat cost $	254.36 1973/1974
Taxes 1974	$1,871.57
Gas ☒	Oil ☐ Coal ☐
Roof shingle	Siding cedar
Sewer ☐	Septic ☒
Water cost $	Well ☒

Rooms/Floor	1	2	3	B	Size
Living	X				14' X 22'
Dining	X				12'6" X 14'
Dining	Comb. ☐ "L" ☐ Separate ☒				
Kitchen	X				12' X 19 (a)
Baths	X	X			cabana on 1st floor
Family Room	X				14'5" X 21' (b)
Den	X				12' X 14'
Utility Room	X				7'9" X 14'
Mr. Brm.		X			14' X 20'11" (c)
Brm. No. 2		X			10'6" X 14'
Brm. No. 3		X			11'7" X 12'
Brm. No. 4		X			12' X 12'
Brm. No. 5					
Foyer	X	X			13' X 13' 2 story
Theater			X		31'4" X 13' (movie)
Closet (c)		X			5' X 14' (walk-in)

Central Air →	Humidifer Auto-flo
Carpeting	Plush carpeting throughout
Dishwasher	Frigidaire Imperial
Disposal	Frigidaire FDFG
Drapes	Throughout - except #2 + #3
Fireplace	Brick - 4' arched opening
Garage	2½ car — 21' X 21'
Patio	17' X 50' + 10' 34'
Porch Courtyard	17'3" X 21'
Oven/range	Frididaire Built-in ☒
Stove Balcony	(C) 4' X 14'
Storms/screens	Thermopane + screens
Water Softener	☒ Owned ☐ Rented ☐

smoke and fire alarm system
Burglar alarm system
(a) includes generous eating area
(b) with Cathedral beamed ceiling

Basement: Full ☒   Partial ☐   Crawl ☒   Slab ☐   Sub-basement ☐   Size: 26'5" X 49'4"

Other inclusions: custom gas fireplace logs. Negotiable items: refrigerators, freezer, washer, dryer, and 16 H.P. tractor plus attachments.

Exclusions: Exclude drapes in 2nd and 3rd bedrooms

Directions: Barrington Rd. to Mundhank Rd., West to Witt Rd., north to Watergate Rd., West to 92 Watergate Rd.

Inspection Procedure: Please Make an Appointment!

Mortgagee: 1st Federal Savings and Loan Association of California

Mortgage Balance $ _____   PITI: $ _____   Rate: _____ %   Term: _____ Yrs. _____

Assumable?   Yes ☐   No ☒   If yes — service charge?

Reason for selling: Relocating

Remarks: Nature paints a masterpiece here each season. This majestic custom home is situated so that practically every room gets a panoramic view of the beautiful lake of the Coves. This 85 acre private lake is perfect for sailing, fishing, swimming, skating, snowmobiling ... an endless vacation right out your back door.

This is the way your "Home Information Form" should look when you mail it to us. Be sure to print clearly. On the following page is a sample of how this form looks after it is typed, laid out and printed.

HOME INFORMATION FORM
This information is believed reliable, but not warranted.

Address	City	State	Zip	Faces	Rooms	Brms.	Baths	Price
92 Watergate, South Barrington,		Ca.	11010	SW	11	4	3	$148,500.

Owner(s) Gerald M. and Sandra J. Steiner

Phone (Bus.) (312) 397-7887
Phone (Res.) (312) 381-1745

Type/Style	2 story / Spanish
Construction	Brick and Frame
Lot Size	151' X 373' - 1.285 acres
Lot Description	Hilly, 8' above lake
Possession	Immediate
Age/Builder	3 yrs. / M.J. Graft, Inc.
Purchase Year	1973
Schools Par.	St. Annes
Schools Pub.	El. Grove Avenue Jr. Middle School H.S. Barrington High School

Condition — Exc. ☒ Good ☐ Fair ☐
Electric — 100 amp ☐ 200 amp ☒
Heat cost $ 254.36   1973/1974
Taxes 1974 $ 1,871.57
Gas ☒ Oil ☐ Coal ☐
Roof Shingle   Siding Cedar
Sewer ☐ Septic ☒
Water cost $ –   Well ☒

Rooms/Floor	1	2	3	B	Size
Living	X				14' X 22'
Dining	X				12'6" X 14'
Dining	Comb. ☐ "L" ☐ Separate ☒				
Kitchen	X				12' X 19' (a)
Baths	X	X			Cabana on 1st floor
Family Room	X				14'5" X 21' (b)
Den	X				12' X 14'
Utility Room	X				7'9" X 14'
Mr. Brm.		X			14' X 20'11" (c)
Brm. No. 2		X			10'6" X 14'
Brm. No. 3		X			11'7" X 12'
Brm. No. 4		X			12' X 12'
Brm. No. 5					
Foyer	X	X			13' X 13' 2 story
Theater			X		31'4" X 13' (movie)
(c)Closet		X			5' X 14' (walk-in)

Humidifier	Auto-Flo
Carpeting	Plush carpeting throughout
Dishwasher	Frigidaire Imperial
Disposal	Frigidaire FDF6
Drapes	Throughout except #2 & #3
Fireplace	Brick + 4' arched opening
Garage	2½ car - 21' X 21'
Patio	17' X 50' + 10' X 34'
Courtyard	17'3" X 21'
Oven/range	Frigidaire Built-in ☒
(c)Balcony	4' X 14'
Storms/screens	Thermopane + Screens
Water Softener	☒ Owned ☒ Rented ☐

Smoke and Fire Alarm System
Burglar Alarm System
(a) includes generous eating area
(b) with cathedral beamed ceiling

Basement: Full ☒ Partial ☐ Crawl ☒ Slab ☐ Sub-basement ☐ Size: 26'5" X 49'4"

Other inclusions: Custom gas fireplace logs. **NEGOTIABLE ITEMS:** Refrigerators, Freezer, Washer, Dryer, and 16HP Tractor plus Attachments.

Exclusions: Exclude Drapes in 2nd and 3rd Bedrooms.

Directions: Barrington Rd. to Mundhank Rd., West to Witt Rd., North to Watergate Rd., West to 92 Watergate Rd.

Inspection Procedure: Please Make an Appointment!

Mortgagee: 1st Federal Savings and Loan Association of Ca.

Mortgage Balance $ – **PITI:** $ – **Rate:** – % – **Term:** – **Yrs.** –

Assumable? Yes ☐ No ☒ If yes – service charge?

Reason for selling: Relocating

Remarks: Nature paints a masterpiece here each season. This majestic custom home is situated so that practically every room gets a panoramic view of the beautiful LAKE OF THE COVES. This 85 acre private lake is perfect for sailing, fishing swimming, skating, snowmobiling ... an endless vacation right out your back door

7

Creative Advertising

The purpose of this chapter is to make the job of selling your home a little easier as well as a lot more fun. One of the hardest jobs in the world is to sit down and write a new and exciting ad about real estate. When you read through the classified section of your Sunday newspaper, it seems that the same house is for sale all over town. The same colorless phrases describe them all.

Your ad must be read to be acted on. In order to be read it must attract the attention of your prospective buyers. How do you accomplish this? Flag down your readers with an ad that screams for attention. Make your message stand out from all the others on the page. Make it unusual. Employ a new twist or unique appeal that is fresh and provocative. Don't be afraid to let your imagination go. Oftentimes the eyecatching and unconventional will catch the reader's fancy.

Make sure your attention-getting ad has a purpose and offers something desirable. Always remember that people buy benefits or ideas, not things. Your prospective buyer is not buying 14,000 bricks and 8,000 feet of 2"x4"s, he's purchasing a way of life. He buys what your home will do for him and his family. When people change their way of life, they usually change homes also. When a family gets larger, so does their home. When a man acquires financial success, he wants a home with the outward appearances that indicate his achievements and status. Therefore, be certain you ad reflects the way of life your home offers.

Also, basic psychology shows that people like to be identified individually even though they want to be accepted as part of a group. So above all, talk *to* your prospective buyer, not *at* him or around him. The word "YOU" cannot be over-used in advertising!!!

Without making an extensive study of the general subject of advertising, you can readily recognize that the greater part of the advertising you will be doing must be absorbed through the eyes of the general public. The classified ads in the Sunday newspaper, the "Home For Sale By Owner" sign on your front lawn, the direct mailing of the "Home Information Form" — all of these things produce a reaction as a result of being seen. The first principle of "Home" advertising is to catch the eye. No matter how fabulous your home is, no matter how much care may have been taken in the composition of the ad or how important the message is, unless it

catches the eye it will never be read. Therefore, the first principle of advertising is to attract attention.

Secondly, the advertisement must arouse interest. It must stir the reader's emotions or awaken his intellectual curiosity sufficiently to cause him to follow the ad from start to finish. The ad must present more than commonplace statements or mere statistics, such as sizes; it must be interesting and it must be human.

The third principle of advertising is to arouse desire. It is poor advertising that leaves the reader without feeling or emotion. Mere curiosity is not enough. The desire that has been aroused must be strong enough to force the reader to investigate further and to lead him to the next step, which results in action. It is action that successful creative advertising seeks. Your ads are a success when they make your phone ring and there is a prospective buyer on the other end of the line.

Every advertisement should be honest. This sounds like an obvious maxim, but it's very true. Quite often an advertisement that almost condemns the home does more to sell it than an advertisement written in beautiful glowing terms. Many of my real estate associates have discovered this, and examples of such advertising are continually being reprinted in various real estate magazines.

Always frame your advertisement from the buyer's point of view. You know all the reasons why you want to sell your home, but obviously that is of no interest to a prospective buyer. Before you sit down to write the copy, decide what type of person or family would be most interested in buying your home and then write your message directly to him. Be sure to direct your ad to some human interest or instinct. Every home has something that may be made the "desire motivation." Decide what it is and write an ad with that as the central theme. As a result, the copy will present one cohesive, and comprehensive idea rather than a garbled bunch of nonentities. The following are some examples of instinctive appeals your copy should develop:

(1) *Love.* It makes the world go round and it also sells homes. A house is a man's visible statement of his love for his wife and also his hope for future favors. "She will really love you if you sign here on the dotted line."

(2) *Pride of ownership.* Appeal to the prospective buyer who yearns for the satisfaction of owning a home or perhaps likes to putter, build or have a garden.

(3) *Security.* Many people are moving away from the inner-city because they fear being mugged, molested or murdered. Assuming the aforementioned problems are not common occurrences in your neck of the woods, this could create an instinctive appeal for your home in the mind of a prospective buyer presently plagued by such plights.

(4) *Equity and appreciation.* The best way to fight inflation is by owning a home. Your home increases in value faster than our government can destroy the purchasing power of the dollar.

(5) *Parenthood.* Use of parental motivation can be successfully directed to families with school-age children. Is your home near parks, schools or pools? If so, advertise it as a place where happy childhood memories are instilled.

(6) *Comfort* Everybody wants labor-saving and time-saving devices so they can bask in the noonday sun. Do you have a home-owners' association that takes care of exterior painting, landscaping and general maintenance of common areas? Or does your home have a maintenance-free exterior — brick, aluminum siding, etc.? Is there a den or study where one can close out the world for a few fleeting moments?

(7) *Prestige* A costlier home should be advertised with the prestige motivation in mind, as should homes on "important" streets or in "important" subdivisions. The buyer's need to show everyone his wealth can easily be the main reason he will purchase your home.

■ Using the following section as a reference source, you will find writing an ad that screems for attention as easy as 1-2-3. Headline, plus descriptive phrases (be sure to include the number of bedrooms, asking price and telephone number), plus closing phrase — that's all there is to it! You now have an ad with more appeal than 99 per cent of your competition in the Sunday classified.

▶ 1

HEADLINES

☐ It's the extras . . .

☐ Let the March winds blow!

☐ A bargain like this goes in two days.

☐ Clip this ad . . .

☐ Next week may be too late!

☐ Isn't this where you want to be?

☐ It's a dog . . .

☐ Don't fence me in!

☐ Willing to do some HOMEWORK?

☐ The ugly duckling . . .

☐ An exceptional neighborhood!

☐ Gracious, spacious living . . .

☐ A dream house come true!

☐ Children are welcome!

☐ This salt box is sweet as sugar . . .

☐ Starting out? Or slowing down?

☐ Lock the world out . . .

☐ Home For Sale By Owner

☐ Comfort . . .

☐ Prestige . . .

☐ Act Now!

☐ Location . . .

☐ Super Sharp . . .

☐ Pride of Ownership . . .

☐ The grass is greener on this side of the fence . . . all 2 acres of it!

☐ Summer vacations free! Sports galore just minutes away.

☐ You're in luck! You can assume this low, low mortgage . . .

☐ Live Modern!

☐ A love affair is inevitable when you see this 4-bedroom ranch . . .

☐ "Do it yourself" bargain!

☐ Here's a pool with a view . . . and a beautiful house to go with it!

☐ A haven for Dad and the kids . . .

☐ Attention busy executives!

☐ Handymen! Here's a built-in workshop!

☐ Look Mom . . . no steps! Here's a one-floor ranch that makes life easier . . .

☐ Two bedrooms . . . just right for the retired couple

☐ Want to be in the swim? Try this shaded ranch with a marvelous swimming pool in the back.

☐ Family breakfast or formal dinner party . . . you'll love the spaciousness.

☐ Sunbathe in privacy on this huge patio.

☐ Sunshine streams in . . .

☐ Why go away for summer?

☐ Horse Lovers . . .

☐ Here's a challenge . . .

☐ Prettiest on the block . . .

☐ Both town and country . . .

☐ This is nifty if you're thrifty!

☐ Swimming, fishing, boating . . .

☐ Down with taxes!

☐ Outdoor entertaining?

☐ What a view!

☐ Nature paints a masterpiece here each season . . .

☐ Love a rock garden?

☐ Hate to Paint?

☐ $ Save the broker's commission $

☐ Economy . . .

☐ Value . . .

☐ Love and Beauty . . .

☐ Security . . .

☐ Perfect for a family seeking a prime location at a realistic price.

☐ Invite your friends to a splash party in this beautiful pool.

☐ An established garden . . .

☐ An address to be proud of!

☐ A honey for the money!

☐ Goodbye, high taxes!

☐ Why be cramped?

☐ Immediate possession!

☐ For fireplace lovers . . .

☐ What a kitchen!

☐ No financing problem . . .

☐ Near everything!

- [ ] What the doctor ordered . . .

- [ ] Dinner is a delight . . .

- [ ] A home that is ageless . . .

- [ ] Mom! The kids won't track in dirt with this room arrangement!

- [ ] Like to be different? Take a look at this romantic fireplace!

- [ ] Imagine! Three full baths . . .

- [ ] Want to live in a glass house?

- [ ] A house to be cherished . . .

- [ ] Built to endure (and to save you money) . . .

- [ ] Bring your green thumb . . .

- [ ] More than you'd expect . . .

- [ ] This beauty isn't wood deep!

- [ ] The upstairs is downstairs . . .

- [ ] Opportunity is knocking!

- [ ] Want a house or a home?

- [ ] Move right in!

- [ ] He who hesitates . . .

- [ ] A romantic fireplace . . .

- [ ] Rent with option to buy!

- [ ] A room for each child . . .

- [ ] Almost cleans itself . . .

- [ ] Late to work no more!

- [ ] C-o-m-f-o-r-t!

- [ ] Wall-to-wall spaciousness . . .

- [ ] Don't wait until dark . . .

- [ ] Grab this fast! It won't last!

- [ ] All on one floor!

- [ ] Priceless charm!

- [ ] 2 minutes walk to everything . . .

- [ ] Key to heaven . . .

- [ ] Comfort is what counts!

- [ ] Away from it all!

- [ ] Enjoy fall's full splendor in this woodsy setting.

- [ ] Before winter winds howl, be settled and cozy in this home.

- [ ] We buried the hatchet and saved all the beautiful trees.

- [ ] Good old summertime will mean more in this lovely home.

☐ Bring along your hammer . . .

☐ A morning swim . . .

☐ For the man who wants everything . . .

☐ Take over from an experienced gardener . . .

☐ Looks like a butler would answer . . .

☐ Love to cook?

☐ What a stately staircase!

☐ Even your cat will purr . . .

☐ The perfect, cozy home for your family's way of life.

☐ Nice evergreen plantings stay pretty and green all year.

☐ The garden is eager to bloom around this lively home.

☐ Welcome sweet springtime at the door of this bright new home.

☐ Wondering what to do with the kids this summer? Turn'em loose in the pool.

☐ Enjoy watching spring unfold in this picturesque hillside setting.

☐ A nature lover's haven . . . just in time to cure spring fever.

☐ No spring cleaning in this immaculate home.

☐ No more sizzling summers in this centrally air-conditioned home.

☐ Year-round vacation home you won't want to leave.

☐ Give your children the advantage of this home in an area of new, uncrowded schools.

☐ Way below reproduction cost!

☐ Transferred owner must bid his home a hasty good-by; priced low to speed the sale.

☐ Come in after church Sunday.

☐ Values like this sell quickly, so call today.

☐ Don't be disappointed by a "Sold" sign . . .hurry out now!

☐ Come early!

☐ You're invited to our Open House!

▶ 2

DESCRIPTIVE PHRASES

■ LIVING ROOM

○ Gracious living area allows easy furniture arrangements.

○ Gracious, spacious living room provides lavish entertainment area.

○ A woman's dream, it allows many furniture arrangement variations.

○ Living room overlooks beautiful yard.

○ A living room for the fun-loving family.

○ A unique living room that decorators dream about.

○ If you like open living, this living room was designed for you.

○ Relax and dream in this elegant living room.

○ Fascinating bay-front living room.

○ Dramatic sunken living room.

○ Entertainment-size living room with fireplace.

○ Ideally suited for dramatic furniture arrangements.

○ Exposed-beam living room has lovely hill-side view.

○ Air of gracious formality in this living room.

○ Living room has cathedral ceiling.

○ A perfect place for a piano.

○ Open balcony overlooking living room.

○ Living room highlighted by spiral staircase.

○ Brick fireplace adds cozy feeling to living room.

○ Bay-window living room adds light, airy effect to home.

○ Dramatic sunken living and dining rooms for elegant entertaining.

○ Large sunken living room you'll love to arrange and friends will envy.

○ Air of gracious formality in this living room created by decorator wallpaper and chandelier.

○ "Great Hall" living room has cathedral ceiling with open beams.

○ Gracious arched doorways in living room.

○ Cathedral ceiling living room where you'll entertain proudly.

■ DINING ROOM

◇ Gracious dining room begs for candlelight.

◇ Informal dining room adds charm to entertaining.

◇ Proudly entertain hubby's business associates in this elegant dining room.

◇ Enjoy the cheerful comfort of the sunny, family-sized dining room.

◇ The dining room radiates warmth for family and guests.

◇ Entertain in uncrowded comfort in this spacious dining area.

◇ A formal dining room with high ceiling just right for candlelight.

◇ Seating 12 is no problem in this big dining room.

◇ Dining room can be closed off completely with sliding doors.

◇ Lush carpeting adds graciousness to entertaining in this formal dining room.

◇ Functional living room/dining room arrangement.

◇ Sunny dining room.

◇ Kitchen and patio dining area.

◇ Formal dining room opens onto patio.

◇ Convenient! Only a step to the kitchen.

◇ This cheery dining space makes meal time a happy occasion.

◇ A dining room that puts graciousness back into entertaining.

◇ Step-saving dining "L".

◇ This dining room will take the largest table.

◇ Room for your buffet and china cabinet, too.

◇ Garden-view dining.

■ BEDROOMS

○ Spacious master bedroom with private tiled bath.

○ Quiet separate bedroom wing for restful sleeping.

○ Convenient bath and dressing room just off master bedroom.

○ Child's bedroom designed for growing and dreaming.

○ Master bedroom with private bath.

○ Bedrooms grouped around center hall.

○ You will be pleased with the size of the bedrooms.

○ Bedrooms overlook trees and garden.

○ You'll want to sleep longer in this restful bedroom.

○ Sun deck off master bedroom.

○ Real fireplace in master bedroom.

○ Sleep like a baby in these air-conditioned bedrooms.

○ Separate his and her bedroom closets.

○ Ideally planned upstairs hall that moves breezes through every bedroom.

○ Room for twin beds and then some.

○ Recessed bedroom windows offer a quaint effect and double as enjoyable window seats.

○ Cool-blue bedrooms that make sleep easy.

○ Fireplace in master bedroom for those cozy winter nights.

○ Dormitory style bedrooms where your children will have plenty of room to study.

○ Perfect nursery . . . quiet, secluded from living areas.

○ Luxurious master bedroom adjoined by bath and dressing room.

○ Your little Miss America will love the mirrored door and big closets in her "Sweet Dream" room.

○ Stately master bedroom decorated tastefully.

○ Three cheery bedrooms in sleep-inducing pastels.

○ Upstairs bedroom and bath give privacy of separate apartment.

○ Sunny east exposure greets early risers.

○ Luxurious master bedroom accommodates the most lavish furnishings.

○ Three bright, cross-ventilated bedrooms for cool summer living.

○ Many-windowed bedrooms overlook garden.

○ Master bedroom with mirrored wall gives you that spacious, open feeling.

○ Out of bed and into the pool . . . what a way to start a day.

○ Bedroom with bath on first floor solves your in-law problem.

◯ Three bright, cross-ventilated bedrooms.

◯ First-floor bedroom with sliding-door, walk-in closets. Serves dual purpose as guest room or study.

◯ Restful, away-from-the-street bedroom.

◯ Luxury-size bedrooms.

■ KITCHEN

◇ Bright, cozy breakfast room for memorable family get-togethers.

◇ Breakfast in this warm, cheerful corner is a real family treat.

◇ Spacious breakfast room doubles as dining room.

◇ Cheerful breakfast corner for neighborly get-togethers.

◇ Step-saving breakfast bar for Mother's busy mornings.

◇ Brimming with feminine appeal and warm "livability."

◇ Kitchen with every automatic control available gives you built-in maid service.

◇ Huge kitchen gives you happy spot for menu planning, telephoning and TV viewing.

◇ Tastefully decorated kitchen has ample cabinets plus built-in burners and oven.

◇ Cozy, eat-in kitchen both Mom and family will enjoy.

◇ A kitchen where the whole family can sit down and eat together.

◇ Big, family-size kitchen with utility room and adjacent "mud" room to eliminate tracking up your clean floors.

◇ Sun-drenched breakfast area.

◇ Joyous work-saving kitchen with cozy breakfast nook.

◇ Meal preparing is a breeze in the ultramodern kitchen.

◇ Kitchen has built-ins and modern conveniences galore.

◇ Honeymoon breakfast nook.

◇ Disposal and dishwasher let you dash away after dinner.

◇ You don't need roller skates in this kitchen — everything within arm's reach.

◇ This all-electric kitchen makes cooking really fun.

◇ A step-saving kitchen without the crowded feeling.

◇ The warmth of fine wood cabinets.

◇ Well-planned kitchen has storage space galore.

◇ Decorator's dream kitchen that makes cooking a pleasure.

◇ Just oodles of cupboard space.

◇ This well-organized kitchen will be the center of the home.

◇ Kitchen has gadgets galore.

◇ Yes, an island in the kitchen.

◇ Pleasant easy-to-work-in kitchen with everything built in.

◇ A kitchen every mother will love.

◇ Big family-size kitchen with adjacent "mud" room.

◇ Oversize sunny kitchen with natural wood cabinets and breakfast nook.

◇ Spill-proof breakfast room for your little "eager eaters."

◇ A dazzling kitchen with every conceivable built-in.

◇ Island kitchen with beautiful breakfast area.

◇ Beautiful, sparkling kitchen has built-in stove and oven.

◇ Step-saving kitchen makes cooking simple.

◇ Colorful kitchen with over-the-sink window.

◇ Perky modern kitchen with cozy breakfast corner.

◇ Older kitchen with lots of room and endless possibilities.

■ BATH

○ No shower shivers — instant wall heater at your fingertips.

○ Full bath located off hallway to serve three bedrooms.

○ You'll feel like a queen in this large luxurious bath!

○ Two complete tiled baths so you and the kids can leave home on time in the morning.

○ Spacious first-floor powder room to please your guests.

○ Out of bed and into a walk-in shower . . . what a way to start a day.

○ His and her sinks . . . no waiting to shave in this bathroom.

○ Wait no more . . . 2½ large bathrooms to serve everyone.

◇ Vanity in bath number one...glass shower enclosure in bath number two.

◇ See this simply gorgeous tiled bath-shower enclosure with sliding glass doors.

◇ Ceramic-tile baths and floors make cleaning easy.

◇ Both baths connect with bedrooms!

◇ Almost room to swim in the bathroom.

◇ "Kid-proof" tiled bathroom.

◇ A two-at-a-time-in-privacy bathroom design.

◇ Gleaming tile bathrooms.

◇ One bath — but a big one, all modern.

◇ Safety bottom tub with adjustable overhead shower and sliding-door shower enclosure.

■ DEN/LIBRARY

◇ An "at home" study hall for young scholars.

◇ Happiness for Dad is relaxing in this lion-sized den.

◇ Sound-proof den for the busy executive who needs an office at home.

◇ Spacious den with extra-guest-room potential.

◇ Quiet retreat for adults who enjoy good books and good music.

◇ Paneled den for hobbies or hubby's retreat.

◇ Attractive den can be extra sleeping room if needed.

◇ No more late nights at the office...Dad can work at home in this cozy den.

◇ A den that's a homework haven for Dad and the kids.

◇ Den is a hideaway for parents.

◇ Office-at-home for a busy executive.

◇ This handy sewing room can be Mom's workshop.

◇ Entire wall of bookshelves provides character and easy access to books.

◇ Beautiful mahogany paneling and two walls of bookshelves in the library.

■ BASEMENT

◇ Big, flood-proof basement.

◇ Everything ready to install a basement bathroom.

○ Extra basement room can easily be converted into an at-home office.

○ Handy outside entrance to daylight basement.

○ Immaculate, bright basement ideal for recreation room.

■ FAMILY ROOM

◇ Family room play center keeps the rest of the house neat.

◇ Family room just right for teenage parties.

◇ Kid-proof family room where little ones can "live a little."

◇ Favorite spot for family fun and informal entertaining.

◇ Tiled floor and paneled walls make this family room "party proof."

◇ Handy sewing room.

◇ Family room play center keeps the rest of the house neat.

◇ Child-proof family room where everyone can "live a little" without concern.

◇ Small enough to care for easily; large enough for entertaining.

■ UTILITY ROOM

○ Large "mud" room and utility room combined.

○ Utility room has additional space for workshop and laundry.

○ Wash day is almost fun in this bright utility room.

○ Ideal utility room.

○ Handy clothes chutes to washer-dryer.

■ CLOSETS

◇ Enormous 7-foot sliding-door bedroom closets.

◇ Louvered closet doors provide constant ventilation.

◇ Jumbo closets store all your bulky items with ease.

◇ No groping, each closet is well lighted.

◇ Mirrored folding closet doors.

◇ A special closet for toys and other extras.

◇ King-sized walk-in closets so clothes are never crushed and wrinkled.

◇ The closets are a housewife's dream.

◇ Scads of storage space.

◇ Abundant closet space.

◇ Enjoy the convenience of wall-to-wall sliding closet doors.

◇ Jumbo closets.

◇ Space galore in these big closets.

◇ Big closets for the kids too.

◇ Big walk-in closets.

◇ Nice big coat closet off of flagstone entry hall.

◇ No groping in these lighted closets.

◇ Priceless protection of cedar-lined closets.

■ ENTRANCES

○ A walk to the front door is like a walk through the woods.

○ Colonial pillars give your entrance a touch of elegance.

○ A home planned around center entry hall.

○ Curved stairway graces entrance hall.

○ Dramatic two-story foyer.

○ Flagstone path curves gracefully to front door.

○ Enclosed garden foyer provides serene atmosphere.

■ DECORATIVE EXTRAS

◇ Completely redecorated . . . just move in.

◇ Tasteful draperies and carpeting go with house.

◇ Glowing hardwood trim.

◇ Louvered doors add decorator touch.

◇ Brass hardware enhances every room.

◇ If you like antiques you'll find this house perfectly suited to them.

◇ Full-length sliding glass doors lead to adjoining garden.

◇ Has handsome cove molding found only in the well-built homes.

◇ Sparkling crystal chandelier.

◇ Unique wallpaper design gives that open-space feeling.

◇ Freshly decorated, ready for you to move in immediately.

■ HEATING AND AIR CONDITIONING

○ A house that promotes better health . . . radiant heat for winter, air-conditioning for summer.

○ The clean, even comfort of automatic gas, forced-air heating.

○ Whole house air-conditioned . . . defies hottest summer.

○ Natural-gas heat provides clean, economical comfort.

○ Dustless, year-round comfort from this heating-cooling system.

○ Radiant heat . . . nothing to interfere with your furniture.

○ Automatic oil furnace . . . last word in economy.

■ FIREPLACES

◇ Magnificent stone fireplace . . . the center of cheerful gatherings.

◇ Your family will love the wood-burning fireplace's glow.

◇ The big, cozy fireplace warms peaceful winter nights.

◇ You will enjoy many quiet nights by this attractive old-brick fireplace.

◇ Dramatic fireplace adds decorator's touch.

◇ Stretch out on the soft carpet and watch the flames dance up the chimney.

◇ Enjoy the warmth of the see-through fireplace from either the living room or the dining room.

◇ Gather round this beautiful fireplace and create childhood memories that will be a part of your children's life forever.

◇ Fireplace adds cozy note.

◇ Raised-hearth fireplace is conversation piece.

◇ Enjoy the cozy charm of a brick fireplace.

◇ More than a decoration, this fireplace is an efficient heating unit.

◇ Massive stone fireplace for warm winter get-togethers.

◇ A warm, friendly fireplace.

◇ Beautiful and modern off-the-floor fireplace.

◇ Your children will love hanging stockings over this fireplace.

◇ Modern, romantic raised fireplace.

■ POOLS

○ Want to be in the swim? A bonus extra is a marvelous swimming pool.

○ Resort luxury in your own backyard with the beautiful swimming pool.

○ The pool is lovely.

○ Delightful swimming pool with cabana.

■ WINDOWS

◇ View the splendor of the countryside through the picture window, while you enjoy the warmth of the romantic fireplace.

◇ Live in an "open world" with sliding window walls.

◇ Free-flowing space enhanced by a glass wall.

◇ Graceful glass to let the outside in.

◇ Insulated windows keep house cooler in summer, warmer in winter.

◇ Removable windows, easy to wash.

◇ Big windows with woodsy view.

◇ Multipaned windows add New England charm.

◇ Panoramic picture window lets in sunshine.

■ FLOORS

○ Wall-to-wall carpeting gives your rooms a luxurious beginning.

○ Glamorous parquet floors set off your area rugs.

○ Elegant hardwood trim and solid oak floors throughout.

○ Beautiful parquet floors add richness to living area.

○ Feet will never get cold in this house . . . carpeted throughout.

○ Lustrous hardwood floors throughout.

○ The finest carpeting, underlaid with foam-rubber padding.

○ Linoleum that looks and wears like stone.

○ Colorful terrazzo floor.

○ Glowing wood floors.

○ Glamorous parquet floors.

○ Dark oak floors enhance this home.

○ Every room in the house is carpeted.

■ CEILING

◇ Drop ceiling adds decorative touch.

◇ Impressive vaulted ceilings.

◇ Beamed ceiling magnifies the warmth and space of this room.

◇ Walnut-stained, beamed ceilings.

◇ High ceilings will accommodate tallest furniture.

◇ Cathedral ceiling gives you that spacious feeling.

■ ELECTRICAL

○ Dramatic electrical fixtures give you light where you need it.

○ Entrance lighting brings a cheerful greeting of gracious hospitality.

○ Designer lighting fixtures for modern "extra touch."

○ Phone outlet jacks wired throughout the house.

○ Keep in touch with the family through the intercom system in every room.

○ Dimmer switches give you the exact amount of light you need.

○ Safe 100-plus wiring.

○ Clean, silent electric heating.

○ Lots of convenient electrical outlets.

○ Soft backyard lighting adds a glow to patio parties.

○ Wired for today's modern electric living.

■ LANDSCAPING

◇ Flower garden is the pride of the neighborhood.

◇ For the birds . . . and perfect for you too, if you enjoy wildlife.

◇ Watch the youngsters while they play.

◇ Nestled on lovely, tree-bordered acre lot.

◇ Half-acre site overlooking scenic, rolling countryside.

◇ The grass is greener on this side of the fence.

◇ Compact yard makes lawn and shrubbery fun instead of work.

◇ Underground sprinkler keeps lawn beautiful.

◇ Manicured lawn.

◇ Very private and very lovely on large, secluded wooded lot.

◇ Picturesque wooded lot.

◇ Sunlit garden.

◇ Circular drive sweeps to your front door.

◇ A fine garden that a little care can make magnificent.

◇ Spring, summer and fall flowers abound in profusion.

◇ Stately trees shade home, stand guard over a spring garden.

◇ Lovely old trees tenderly preserved to enhance home.

◇ Towering elm trees planted for year-round greenery.

■ GARAGE

○ Finished garage interior is further mark of quality.

○ A garage for two cars plus all the bikes, tools and toys you own.

○ Room for your workshop too, in the oversize, heated garage.

○ Heated attached garage — a pleasure on frosty mornings.

○ Automatic electric-eye garage doors save steps.

○ Huge double garage with special storage for good-sized boat or workshop.

■ PATIOS

◇ A lovely terrace under stately trees.

◇ Tree-shaded patio.

◇ Picnic-perfect patio with huge brick barbecue.

◇ Lighted outdoor patio just off the kitchen makes evening entertaining a breeze.

◇ Screened patio lets sun and breeze in . . . keeps pests out.

◇ Day and night patio . . . lighted and screened in for privacy.

◇ For family breakfast or party dinner, you'll enjoy the big patio.

◇ Sheltered cocktail patio.

◇ Sliding doors open onto sun-swept patio.

◇ Stone barbeque invites Dad to cook.

◇ A big, old-fashioned veranda for lovely, lazy summer evenings.

■ LOCATION

○ Friendly neighbors give "hometown" feeling to city living.

○ Where influential families live.

○ Neighborhood of young executives on their way up.

○ Just around a quiet corner from offices and shopping center.

○ Lovely Lincoln Park is close by for family picnics and recreation.

○ Convenient bus service to all areas is two blocks away.

○ Friendly young neighborhood with lots of new friends for your children.

○ Catches warm sun during the day and cool breezes at night.

○ A short, pleasant bus ride to downtown.

○ Let your children live where the trees are tall, the air is pure.

○ Summerville . . . where home values maintain a high level.

○ Cramped and crowded? Enjoy easy living, open air at Summerville.

○ Suburbia at its best. Convenient, secluded Summerville.

○ Just what the doctor ordered; peace, fresh air, sunshine.

○ Centered on three naturally beautiful acres.

○ Professionally landscaped one acre lot looks attractive winter and summer.

○ Beautiful trees and annuals enhance this exquisite one acre lot.

○ Graceful plantings on this acre lot require minimum care.

○ In a splended, wooded section on two acres.

○ In Summerville, restful, pretty section of older well-kept homes.

○ Nestled on a large country plot in beautiful, scenic Summerville.

○ Privacy, yet only a few minutes from shopping.

○ Outdoor area offers choice of a place to sun or a spot to shade.

○ Where everyone wants to live, but few have the opportunity.

○ Schools for tots through teens conveniently located.

○ Picturesque setting of your dreams.

○ Snuggled into a hill.

○ Very tranquil and quiet, only the sound of the breeze.

○ Garden is in full bloom, a riot of color.

○ White pecket fence with a swinging garden gate.

○ Suburbia in the heart of the city, children can romp in their parklike yard.

○ Rolling four acre lot, privacy without isolation.

○ Neighborhood pride is reflected by the immaculate homes throughout the area.

■ ARCHITECTURE

◇ Contempory home designed for an expanding young family.

◇ Cozy Cape Cod to snuggle around your whole family.

◇ Proud colonial with graceful pillars bespeaks your preference for elegance.

◇ Spacious split-level with a distinctive custom quality that reflects your individuality.

◇ Cedar siding gives maintenance-free beauty.

◇ A gleaming-white stucco bungalow, complete with picket fence.

◇ Rambling brick-face ranch, a gracious home with minimum upkeep.

◇ Impressive, gracious colonial exterior.

◇ This decidedly Early American farmhouse is set on very gently rolling acres.

◇ A Garrison home with rich oak trim that gives it a picture-book look.

◇ Rambling colonial with background of Old English hedgerows.

◇ Enchanting Southern-style colonial with stately white pillars and lively green shutters.

◇ Prestige English Tudor set among towering elms.

◇ Clean, cool individual look of Swiss chalet.

◇ Cozy, even to the white-framed casement windows, as only true Cape Cod can be.

◇ Proud Georgian styling in rich brick.

■ COMMUNITY ADVANTAGES

○ As pretty as a private park.

○ In a setting of tranquil charm.

○ A country home your wife will love.

○ Live where you have all city conveniences.

○ Highly rated fire department.

○ Excellent hospital nearby.

○ A child's paradise.

○ No need for two cars in this perfect location.

○ Just a hop, skip and jump from school.

○ Summer vacations are free! Sports galore in this area.

○ A community of fine folks.

○ You'd love to have lived here as a child.

○ Neighborhood pride is reflected in the well-kept homes.

○ Playmates galore for your children in this young community.

○ A community where people care.

○ In a parklike neighborhood of well-kept homes.

○ Peaceful neighborhood.

○ Privately policed.

○ Well-established neighborhood.

○ 24-hour fire and police protection.

▶ 3

CLOSING PHRASES

☐ Delay may mean disappointment; see this unusual offer today!

☐ Dial   right now . . . the most important call you'll make this year.

☐ Don't delay; you may wait too long.

☐ Don't miss the boat!

☐ Don't wait. See it today.

☐ Drastically reduced to sell at once.

☐ For a great home . . . priced right . . . see this outstanding offer!

☐ For full particulars and appointment to inspect call NOW!

☐ If you are interested in an exceptional investment, see this property at once.

☐ If super construction plus a beautifully planned home with spacious rooms and a very reasonable price are appealing to you, do not delay in seeing this home.

☐ Make us an offer today.

☐ Photo and full description mailed on request.

☐ Don't pass up this opportunity. Drive out now!

☐ Call us quick! We're betting it sells today!

☐ It's easy to own this lovely home. VA or FHA financing OK!

☐ A tension-free home of bright, softly carpeted rooms.

☐ Privacy Plus, in this secluded location.

☐ Come see it this afternoon.

☐ An exceptionally nice home open today for your inspection.

☐ Hurry out! It's too good to miss.

☐ Your chance to secure family happiness.

☐ Don't pass up this opportunity. Drive out now!

☐ Call us quick! We're betting it sells today!

☐ It's easy to own this lovely home. VA or FHA financing OK!

☐ A tension-free home of bright, softly carpeted rooms.

☐ Privacy Plus, in this secluded location.

☐ Take advantage of this fine offer now.

☐ There are always more buyers than really good houses for sale . . . so act quickly!

☐ This home is the best value on today's market at only $

☐ Tomorrow will be too late!

☐ Tremendous value, impossible to duplicate at twice the price.

☐ See this home today . . . before it's sold!

☐ Bring your family now to this house of the future.

☐ Come Saturday or Sunday from 10:00 to 4:00. I will be on hand to answer your questions and show you this beautiful home.

☐ Drop what you're doing and come to 92 Upper Pond!

☐ Drive out this afternoon and be charmed.

☐ If you're a serious buyer, get here fast.

☐ Absolutely nothing to do but move in! See it today.

☐ Be our guest . . . open house showing TODAY!

☐ No foolin', I must sell this week.

☐ Since this meets your needs, I recommend quick action!

☐ You may have immediate possession.

☐ Come see it this afternoon.

☐ Promise her anything . . . but buy her this home.

☐ Please, no brokers. I want to save the buyer the exorbitant commission you charge!

☐ Really a fine home that you should see without delay. Phone now for an appointment to inspect.

☐ A beautiful opportunity for YOU.

☐ Act quickly on this genuine bargain.

☐ The answer to your home-hunting problem can be found by phoning today.

☐ At $ there is nothing comparable in comfort, appearance and location.

☐ Better be an early bird.

☐ Building costs have risen so rapidly that it would be impossible to duplicate this home at the price you can buy it for today.

☐ Call for an appointment for a private showing.

☐ Call tonight. Tomorrow may be too late.

☐ Come on over today.

☐ Come out this afternoon — bring your checkbook, I'll be there.

☐ An exceptionally nice home open today for your inspection.

☐ Hurry out! It's too good to miss.

☐ Your chance to secure family happiness.

☐ Priced for quick sale, so call now!

▶ **POWER WORDS**

Most psychologists agree that certain words have an emotional impact on the general public. Certain words almost automatically have a strong appeal, no matter how they're used. Experts in communications have long tried to identify these power words, and their research has now proved to be invaluable to everyone dealing in sales, advertising and politics — actually anyone who is trying to influence other people. The following list is a compilation of the 60 most powerful words. The most persuasive and emotional words are at the beginning. Try to use as many as possible in your advertising and when you're talking to a prospective buyer.

1.	You	31.	Economical
2.	Love	32.	Modern
3.	Money	33.	Elegance
4.	Easy	34.	Sympathy
5.	Health	35.	Necessary
6.	New	36.	Courtesy
7.	Guaranteed	37.	Growth
8.	Save	38.	Versatile
9.	Proven	39.	Obligation
10.	Free	40.	Super
11.	Results	41.	Status
12.	Discovery	42.	Enormous
13.	Beauty	43.	Low-cost
14.	Home	44.	Genuine
15.	Mother	45.	Progress
16.	Value	46.	Thinking
17.	Safe	47.	Excel
18.	Integrity	48.	Engineered
19.	Quality	49.	Recommended
20.	Bargain	50.	Rugged
21.	Scientific	51.	Stylish
22.	Durable	52.	Admired
23.	Clean	53.	Innovation
24.	Efficient	54.	Personality
25.	Time-saving	55.	Independent
26.	Fun	56.	Successful
27.	Ambition	57.	Up-to-date
28.	Reputation	58.	Tested
29.	Stimulating	59.	Relief
30.	Popular	60.	Tasteful

The large metropolitan newspapers are the best place to advertise your home because their readership is so vast. If there's more than one such newspaper in your area, select the one with the largest real estate section. A home buyer will always read the paper with the widest home selection, and that's where you want your ad to be.

The best response day is Sunday and the second best is Saturday. Normally the rest of the week is not worthwhile in relation to the cost. Quite often a newspaper will have a Saturday/Sunday package deal at an appreciable savings. Be sure to check into this.

Try varying the wording of your ad each week to increase your reading audience and the likelihood of finding a buyer. If you receive an extremely good response from one particular ad, then by all means repeat it again.

To properly promote the sale of your residence it will be necessary for you to invest up to 1 per cent of the market value in advertising. Of course, if your home is overpriced you'll have to spend appreciably more to attract a buyer, if you are able to get one at all, because it takes longer and costs more to find a buyer for a $60,000 home than a $30,000 home. The ads for a $60,000 home have to be larger in order to list the various extras and amenities not found in a $30,000 residence.

In the following example ads, the large display ad was put in a small local paper while the smaller ads were placed in a large metropolitan newspaper. The smaller ads cost one-half the price of the large ad but created twice as much interest. It has been my experience that local advertising is wasted. The only reason you see so many real estate firms advertising locally is that they're trying to list more homes in that area. Local real estate advertising is a listing tool, not a home-selling tool! Spend your advertising dollars wisely.

72

8

How to Become a Real Estate Salesman Overnight

The main goal of this book is to assist you in the sale of your home. The purpose of this chapter is to give you a general working knowledge of the procedures involved in real estate selling. It is the exception and not the rule when a home sells itself without any effort on the part of the owner. Benjamin Franklin once said, "The only thing you can achieve without effort is failure."

When working with a prospective buyer, you should have the following attitudes and goals:

(1) *Be enthusiastic.* If you honestly feel that you're selling a terrific home, you'll impart that enthusiasm to the prospect and he'll feel that he's truly buying a terrific home.

(2) *Know your home and the surrounding area.* Use the "Home Information Form" as a handy reference. The buyer is going to have questions on how close the schools are, the age of the furnace, whether the walls are insulated or not, where the property lines are, etc.

(3) *Know your competition.* What are the homes selling for in your area? Why is your home a better buy? Every time you see a "For Sale" sign pop up in your neighborhood, call and ask what the price is and what's included. If possible, arrange to view it. Thereby you'll have a first-hand knowledge of exactly what your local home market is.

(4) *Be a problem solver.* Does your prospect have a special problem or need? Show him how purchasing your home will solve those problems or fill those needs. Does he want a den-library? Explain to him that the fourth bedroom off the living room could easily be converted to this purpose.

(5) *Command respect.* People like to deal with a person they respect and trust. If they don't believe what you're saying, if they don't think you're honest, they'll never buy your home.

(6) *Have a burning desire to sell your home as soon as possible.* Desire is what really rules human action. If you have a "don't-care" attitude, the buyer will sense it and feel that he has all the time in the world to make a decision.

(7) *Size up the buyer.* What motivates him? What type of reasoning will make him sign on the dotted line? The following is a list of personal motivations, some of which are always present in the purchase of real estate:

(a-) Love of luxury
(b) Pride
(c) Imitation — the "Jones's" impulse
(d) Expectation of profit
(e) Pride of possession
(f) Necessity
(g) Ambition
(h) Self-preservation
(i) Vanity
(j) Physical security
(k) Love of wife
(l) Love of family
(m) Financial security for the future
(n) Desire for power
(o) Love of physical comfort
(p) Income for old age
(q) Enhancement of reputation
(r) Companionship
(s) Desire to excel
(t) Desire for leadership
(u) Social prestige
(v) Happiness

When you're looking through the classified section of the newspaper, you'll notice that the vast majority of the home ads stress price. They mention low down payment, high rate of return, appreciation, below market price, etc. It goes without saying that everyone likes a bargain, but for the majority of the home buyers it's not nearly as important as the real estate brokers seem to think.

To most people, the main goal in buying a home is happiness. While appealing to a buyer's sense of economy, a seller must also appeal to his strong need for happiness. Interest is quickly created when a seller makes a prospective buyer realize how much he and his family will enjoy living in the home.

(8) *Use power words.* Review the power words listed in the "Creative Advertising" chapter. Words such as love, beauty, happiness and economy stir interest and create desire.

(9) *Help the prospective buyer say yes.* Ask a question in such a manner that you'll get a positive response instead of a negative one. This is one of the oldest techniques used by the master salesman. Ask a question that the buyer will answer with a "yes." Avoid asking a question that can be answered with a "no."

For example: "Isn't this a lovely, bright living room?" Or "These self-cleaning ovens are a real work saver, aren't they?" Or "There's nothing cheerier than a crackling fire on a cold winter's night, is there?"

Every "yes" answer you get puts you one step closer to the final "yes" you are looking forward to.

(10) *Get the buyer involved.* Have him do things, touch things, look at things and measure things. Every time he actually does something by himself, he's selling himself. His own actions are persuading him to buy.

Have your prospect look at the view through the picture window, pace off the length and width of the lot, open the damper in the fireplace. Have him check the salt level in the water softner and feel the basement wall for dampness. Even let him crawl in the crawl space, assuming it's crawlable. Most experienced, successful salesmen strive to get a prospect into motion. They try to condition a prospect's mind into action by having him say and do things that cause him to become involved. Car salesmen use this technique quite extensively. Remember the last time you sold yourself a car? Didn't the salesman say, "Here are the keys. Get behind the wheel and drive it around the block." The same approach will sell your home.

(11) *Know when to shut up!* Thomas Edison once said that God made the original talking machine and that all Edison did was invent one that could be turned off. Don't get carried away with your own oratory. Know when to be silent. Unnecessary information should not be volunteered, and you should not feel that you have to maintain a constant stream of comments and trivia.

(12) *Attitude is the key to success.* Selling is an attitude not an aptitude. Exude confidence. Feel as though as soon as you have completed talking to this

buyer, you'll be covering your "Home For Sale By Owner" sign with one saying "SOLD." Always talk positively. Never use the word "if" — it implies doubt and uncertainty.

(13) *Use low-pressure finesse.* Since your house suits the buyer's needs, tell him so: "This home is perfect for you and your family. You're going to enjoy living here."

(14) *Recognize buying signals.* When a buyer asks whether or not personal property is being included in the sale of the home, assume he's about to buy. If he asks, "Do the drapes stay?" answer, "Do you want the home if the drapes are included?"

If he asks, "Are the washer and dryer included?" answer, "Do you want the home if we throw in the washer and dryer?"

If he asks, "Can you help me with financing?" answer, "Do you want the home if I can get you financing?"

If he answers "yes" to your question, he has just bought the house.

The sale of your house can be closed when the husband and wife hold short conferences and start whispering, "Well, what do you think honey?" or "You know it would be nice to get out of that apartment before the rent goes up again, or "I think we'll be able to swing it,

don't you?"

(15) *Ask closing questions.* The definition of a closing question is: Any question the answer to which confirms the fact that he has bought. Examples of closing questions are:

"Would you like to move in on the 1st or 15th of May?"

"Would you like to include the refrigerator in your offer?"

"Exactly what items did you want to include in your offer?"

"Should I write a contingency in the contract that it is valid only if your lawyer approves its legal content?"

Important: After you have asked a closing question, SHUT UP!! The next person who talks loses!

(16) *Know how to handle objections.* Usually a prospective buyer will place roadblocks in the way of the seller. He isn't doing this to be malicious but rather to forstall having to make the decision to buy or not to buy. The seller must find out why the prospect does not want to buy before he can attempt to overcome his objections. The seller, not the buyer, is the person who must keep the conversation aimed toward signing the contract.

The basic formula for handling most

objections in real estate sales is as follows: First, agree with the objection by saying "Yes, I understand how you feel." This psychological statement *always* makes the listener feel good and therefore receptive to what you will say next. Second, immediately switch the conversation. Discuss an area of the house he likes very much. And finally, go on selling. For example:

Buyer: This bedroom is too small. My daughter's furniture will never fit in here.

Seller: Yes, I understand how you feel. But you also said that the master bedroom suite was exactly what you were looking for. Your wife really loved the adjoining dressing area. I am sure you'll find the vaulted ceiling very striking.

In order to make sure that you hear everything the buyer is saying and thereby understand what his objection really is, never interrupt him or argue a point. Always allow him enough time to complete his entire statement before you respond, no matter how wrong you think he might be.

Another important area on which objections occur is the matter of price. Always avoid discussing price unless the buyer brings up the subject first. Often it won't even be an issue and you can go ahead and write the contract at the full price suggested by your appraiser. If the buyer won't pay it, you'll find out soon enough. If you discuss price too soon, that becomes the

biggest decision in the sale of your home. Concentrate on selling the benefits of owning your home, not price.

When you and the buyer are in process of negotiating the final price, it's good to remember that most homes sell for less than the seller would like to accept but more than the buyer would like to pay. A fair price is when the buyer doesn't get a bargain and the seller doesn't make a killing. The real art of negotiation is a give and take proposition until an agreeable price has been reached by both parties.

Ninety-five per cent of the time, an interested buyer will make an offer below the asking price. This is something a seller should expect. Let's assume that the appraised value of your home is $50,000 and a prospect comes in with a low-ball figure. What's the best way to handle a situation such as this? Remember, throwing him out is not going to get the house sold. Most likely he's just testing to find out exactly what the rock-bottom price is. The conversation might go something like this:

Buyer: I'm willing to give you $45,000 for this house, and that's the best I can do. Take it or leave it.

Seller: Mr. Smith, I understand how you feel. I can appreciate the fact that you're striving to get the best possible price you can for this home. Since I'm not dealing with you through a real estate broker, you've already saved the 7 per cent commission that I would have had to pay him. It's true that I'm still somewhat flexible in my price and can afford to accept a lower price than the home is appraised at. However, I cannot accept a sale price of $45,000 for this beautiful home. But I'm willing to consider an offer of $49,500.

You should always try to maintain a position from which you can bargain for as long as possible. If, on the other hand, you label any point or condition as being final, it becomes very hard to change your mind at a later time. Swallowing pride is very hard on the ego.

One of the most important phrases in getting a buyer and seller to agree on a final price is "let's split the difference." That way both parties are giving in, but neither has to go more than half way. Splitting the difference changes a $1,000 chasm into a $500 crevice. The closer you get, the better she (the contract) looks.

When a buyer does present an offer, he should accompany it with a 10 per cent earnest deposit to show good faith. Otherwise, there's really nothing to hold the buyer to his side of the bargain. You could hire a lawyer to file a lawsuit to make him fulfill his part of the contract, but it's never worth the time and aggravation. A buyer can practically always get out of a contract to buy real estate — if he so desires and has a sharp real estate attorney.

When negotiating with a buyer, you should maintain control of the conversation by answering a question with a question. In case you're never heard this conversation between the priest and the rabbi, I'll repeat it now:

Father McMahon: Why do you always answer a question with a question?

Rabbi Goldberg: Why do you ask?

The rabbi just gained control of the conversation without divulging any information to the priest.

A prospective buyer might say:

> **Buyer:** I see you're asking $50,000 for this house. What is the lowest price you'll accept?
>
> **Seller:** How much are you willing to offer?
>
> **Buyer:** Oh, I am not sure. Would you take $48,000?
>
> **Seller:** Would you be willing to put that in writing with an earnest deposit?

If the buyer says "no," then you know that he's not really interested and that he's only playing games. Most likely he and his wife go out every Sunday to look at houses just to reassure themselves that their present house is the best deal around. You're wasting your time with this type of person.

On the other hand, if the prospect says, "Yes, I'm willing to put this offer in writing," you know you have a serious buyer who is willing to pay at least $48,000 to purchase your home.

Now you can negotiate in earnest. Remember, you never said you would accept $48,000 for your home. You just wanted to find out if he would put it in writing, thereby proving he was sincere and not just another Sunday driver. Now is the time for you and the buyer to sit down and talk it over. Quite often in the middle of negotiations a roadblock occurs because both parties refuse to budge an inch. For all practical purposes, bargaining has come to a standstill. It is now time for a coffee break. Usually the reason for this impasse is that tension has built up too high. Suggest that the buyer and his wife take a walk in the garden so they can privately review some of the areas of discussion. It's amazing how these 15 minute breaks can work wonders in getting the buyer and seller back on the yellow brick road.

Now let's assume that you have just planted your "Home For Sale By Owner" sign and the first person who comes to the door offers you a fair price for the house. Should you accept it? Positively! You may feel that if you wait the offers will get better, but this isn't necessarily true. All you should expect for your home is a fair price — nothing more, nothing less. On the other side of the coin, the asking price of a home for sale normally declines the longer the home is on the market. Your next offer may not be as good.

When it gets down to the wire (the dotted line), have some personal property (washer, dryer, etc.) in the wings, ready to throw in to sweeten the pot (clinch the sale).

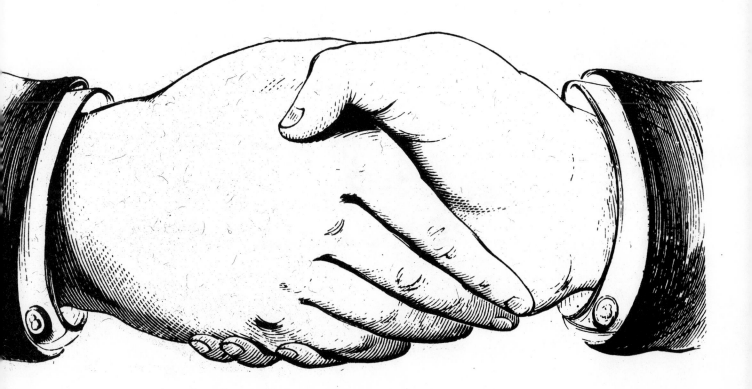

9

The Advantages of Homeownership

Homeownership constitutes to most people an important step in life and undoubtedly represents the most significant single expenditure that will ever be made by the average home buyer. For this reason, the advantages of homeownership should be carefully explored and well understood.

Basically, residential real estate falls into two catagories: (1) houses and (2) homes. A *house* affords the essentials of shelter: it provides adequate protection from the sun, rain, heat and cold. On the other hand, a *home* not only protects against the elements but also offers opportunities for a well-rounded family life, the type of atmosphere that is best suited for the upbringing of healthy, happy children. It is for these reasons that the word "home" and the phrase "way of life" are synonymous.

The ownership of real estate has always been a very strong instinct and desire. It epitomizes the American dream. A recent federal survey shows that 60 per cent of the families in the United States own the home they occupy. Practically everyone would prefer to own a home of their own, thereby building up an equity rather than making a landlord richer by the month. Most families eventually see the light and realize they cannot afford to rent, paying out their hard earned money without getting any return. They're lining someone else's pocket when they could be getting a return on an investment.

Few families purchase their "dream home" the first time around, primarily because of budget considerations. But everyone has to start somewhere, and even the purchase of a modest home is better than paying rent, where all you get in exchange is a piece of worthless paper.

Frequently a prospective buyer doesn't realize how easy it actually is to buy a home of his own. Possibly he has the distorted idea that a large down payment is required. Or possibly he is not sure that his income is substantial enough to cover the monthly mortgage payments. Here's where the expertise of a loan officer is of great value. He can come up with the facts and figures that will greatly assist a buyer in such a situation.

There are many compelling reasons for homeownership. The most important advantages are as follows:

(1) *Security.* The homeowner is secure. World conditions may change, the economy may go up or down, but as long as he meets his mortgage payments he'll have a roof over his head an no one can disturb him. He'll never be subject to an eviction notice. On the other hand, the renter is always insecure. His rent may go up or his landlord may want to evict him. He is not the master of his own ship.

(2) *Savings.* The purchase of a home is equivalent to setting up a savings plan. Most people, myself included, encounter difficulty in establishing a concrete and systematic savings program for themselves. An owner of real estate must make a monthly mortgage payment and therefore learns to be thrifty. He knows money has to be set aside to meet these obligations. Quite often meeting the mortgage payment on a home is the only savings plan of medium and low-income groups.

(3) *Community spirit.* A strong sense of civic pride is one of the results of home-ownership. The homeowner's community participation is normally greater than that of non-homeowners. Therefore, the degree to which an individual actually engages in the organized civic activities of his community usually correlates directly with his homeownership.

When a homeowner is affected by an action of the government, he reacts to it; and sooner than he realizes, the homeowner develops a feeling of being "needed" that induces him to take an active part in civic affairs.

(4) *Credit.* The homeowner who systematically makes his mortgage payment is recognized as a stable and responsible member of his community. This homeowner's credit rating can be counted on as a valuable financial asset whenever he might need it in the future.

(5) *Goals.* Many people wander aimlessly. They have no real goal or purpose in life. Purchasing a home gives them the stimulus they so desperately need: something to work for, a reason to succeed.

(6) *Independence.* Indeed, it is a great feeling for the owner of a home to stand on a plot of ground he can call his own. He is king of his castle even though his realm may be modest. He has no landlord to restrict his activities.

(7) *Peace of mind.* As a homeowner comes closer to paying off his residence, it becomes a truly wonderful refuge from the woes of the world, an isolated island where he can find true peace of mind.

(8) *Happiness.* If a home fits the owner's physical and mental needs, it can only bring great joy. It becomes a place where the children can play to their hearts' content without any complaint from landlords; a place where he can entertain his friends; and a place where he can do the things a tenant may be prohibited from doing.

(9) *Room for hobbies.* Owning a home gives you the opportunity and place to let your unutilized ideas reach fruition. Your wife no longer has to be a latent gardener; at last she can put her green thumb to work. What manner of man hasn't felt the beck and call of building a boat in the basement?

(10) *Fight inflation.* Homeownership represents one of the best ways to beat inflation for most Americans. You can buy a home today, use it for years to come, and sell it at an appreciated value!

(11) *Investment.* Historically, the value of housing has outperformed the stock market (especially since 1968). The purchase of a home is and has been a prudent way to invest your hard-earned, shrinking dollars. Unlike most other investments (stock, bonds, etc.), a home can be enjoyed while you own it. (Have you ever heard of anyone having a stock-warming party?)

(12) *Tax advantages.* The mortgage interest and property taxes you pay on your home are all tax-deductible items. This means that you will pay less for your home than you think. If you are in the 25 per cent bracket, Uncle Sam will refund 25 per cent of all the interest you pay on your home, plus refund 25 per cent of all the taxes you pay on your home. Actually, you won't receive a refund check for this amount. Uncle Sam works on a debit and credit basis,

and therefore the refund is applied to any other taxes you might owe. Even though you never see this money, the savings are appreciable.

Along with the advantages listed above, there will be many other things that the homeowner himself will prize, such as the backyard picnics, the first Christmas and Thanksgiving dinner with room for the relatives.

10

Showing Your Home

When a buyer calls for information on your home, it's important for you to remember that he's actually looking for a reason why he shouldn't bother seeing your home. Always talk positively about the amenities of your home! If a prospect brings up a negative point, always counter it with a positive point:

Buyer: I don't think your house will suit us. We need four bedrooms.

Seller: The den has a closet and can easily be converted into the fourth bedroom you need. And the rest of our house really has to be seen to be appreciated.

Your first contact with the potential buyer will most likely be on the telephone. It's very important for you to keep a copy of the "Home Information Form" near the phone so that you'll be able to control the conversation by offering more information than requested. If you're hesitant about answering questions, the buyer will think you're trying to hide a serious defect and will most likely decide not to view your home because he distrusts you. Always try to gain the buyer's confidence. When you're talking on the phone, always have a smile on your face and your voice will automatically smile.

It should take about 30 minutes or less to properly show your home. Try to book showing appointments about 45 minutes apart. But expect to get "no-shows." These animals are very common and can actually account for 50 per cent of the appointments.

The following is an example of effective question/answer responses between buyer and seller. All you have to do is insert the actual information about your home and you'll have the heart of a telephone conversation that will cover 99 per cent of your inquiries. Most real estate salesmen have a list by their desk of question/answer responses so that they're never caught off guard. You can do the same by listing the important information about your home and by being sure to use the descriptive phrases included in the "Creative Advertising" chapter. This will greatly brighten your conversation, and the buyer, as a result, will actually look forward to viewing your home.

Seller: Hello

Buyer: Hello, I am calling about the home you advertised in the Sunday Trib.

Seller: (SMILE!) Yes. I'm glad you called. It's a very beautiful eight-room ranch with four large bedrooms and 2½ baths. This home is designed with a center hall entry, creating a perfect traffic pattern. There is a delightful Florida room which overlooks the professionally landscaped grounds. Also, we have a lovely terrace under stately trees that give complete privacy and cool breezes in the summer. Would you like to come over to see it?

Buyer: Yes, I would.

Seller: Good. The address is 4307 North Bernard. We'll be home for the rest of the day and will look forward to seeing you. My name is Mark Hopkins. May I ask what your name is?

Buyer: My name is Chuck Smith. My wife and I should be there around 3:00.

You can rest assured that Chuck Smith is glad he called you. He was greeted as a friend and made to feel comfortable. Because of this, he'll feel at ease when he visits your house.

If Chuck Smith had decided not to see your home, it would have been a good idea to send him a copy of the "Home Information Form" anyway. It's always possible for a buyer's needs to change overnight, and if he has your "Home Information Form" handy, he could still be a good prospect. Get these forms in front of as many potential buyers as possible.

When your doorbell rings, compose yourself, put a warm, glowing, genuine smile on your face, and open the door and greet him as though he is an important guest. Make him feel at home! First, introduce yourself and then hand your prospective buyer a "Home Information Form." Tell him it will be your pleasure to give him the Grand Tour of your home. (I don't think it's a good idea to let him wander through your home on his own.) When showing him the home, it's important for you to realize that the prospective buyer wants to open every door and look into practically every cabinet, but he's afraid to because it's not his home. It's up to you to be sure to open all doors and cabinets. The buyer will feel at ease if nothing is being hidden.

Also, remember not to get bogged down talking about subjects not relevant to the sale of your home. Buyers aren't interested in your bowling trophies. Discuss schools, neighbors (the nice ones only), parks, and all the positive points of the house. When you mention price, be sure to tell the buyer how the market value was decided upon — that you actually hired an appraiser who then determined the fair market price (at this moment show him the appraisal). This procedure normally eliminates "low balling" because the buyer is confident that he is not being taken. His first offer will tend to be much more realistic.

While you are still at the front door, give your prospective buyer a rough idea of the general layout so that he'll know what to expect as he tours your home. Since a house consists primarily of space, the floor plan is its most basic feature. While showing the buyer through, make each room mean rest, relaxation, contentment and comfort; he will then want to make the home part of his life.

Good points to enumerate on are efficient usage of space, plentiful storage, linen closets, outdoor living areas, fireplaces and any other amenities that distinguish your home as being carefully planned. As your guide the way, let the buyer select the features of most interest to him, then expound on them. Tell him you'll be happy to answer any questions he might have and that you're interested in any comments he might have, both good and bad. This type of a conversation will give you an insight into his actual needs and wants and into whether he is really able to afford a home such as yours. Also, you'll have the opportunity to answer any questions he might have, which, left unanswered, will easily turn into silent objections that could readily kill a potential sale. Always dispel objections as early in the potential sale as possible, rather than at a less advantageous, later time.

When you've decided exactly what the buyer wants, focus on it. If his wife remarks that she likes the larger kitchen, be sure she knows the dimensions. Pace it off just to dramatize the size. Be sure to have him visualize his family living there — right in that very room. Mention various possible arrangements and locations for the TV set, stero, couch, etc.

Sell the buyer on his own ideas, not on what you think he might like. Let him tell you what he is looking for, and then convince him that he has found it.

Be sure to give the buyer credit for having an ounce of intelligence. As you enter a room don't say "this is the kitchen" or "this is the bathroom." With this type of an introductory phrase, most people feel as though they've just been insulted. Instead, have something descriptive to say about each room: "This kitchen has a self-cleaning oven," or "This bathroom has a heat lamp in the ceiling so that you'll be comfortable when you get out of the shower."

Always sell the benefits of your home, not the physical features. You'll have a tendency to say, "This home is well insulated," and your buyer will think, "So what?" Instead, you should say, "Since this home is so well insulated, it stays cooler in the summer and warmer in the winter. Also, our heating and cooling bills are very low."

If you have an older home, mention the fact that building costs have risen dramatically in just the past years: most of the newer homes have much smaller rooms; therefore, the buyer is getting a lot more for his money when he buys your home.

If your home is newer, mention the many built-in features and conviences that will make their life more comfortable. Stress the fact that it will be many years before they have to make any repairs; they can just sit back and enjoy their home.

Always be sure that the prospective buyer understands the full value of your home. Walk the property line with him, point out the scenic views, call attention to the cedar-shake roof, show him how the intercom system works, etc.

Now here comes the hard part; and you're not going to want to take my advice, but if you don't you'll very probably kill the sale of your home. Point out the faults in your home! If the buyer is going to notice something wrong or detrimental, it's always best for you to mention it first and turn it into a selling feature. Is your kitchen too small? Describe it as a "step-saving" kitchen, convenient and compact yet big enough for all the modern appliances, but with no wasted space. If there is a structural defect, be sure to have at least one bona fide written estimate of the cost to do the necessary repairs. Otherwise the buyer will make a mental estimate at least two to three times more than the actual cost would be.

Be sure to make your prospective buyer feel at home. Relax, don't rush. While showing your home, pause each time he wants to look at some feature closely. Never rush. Let him get the feel of your home. After you have shown a potential buyer through your home, invite him to sit down in your living room and have a cup of coffee. That way he feels a part of your home, not like somebody just passing by.

Be enthusiastic when you're discussing your home. This enthusiasm will be transmitted to the buyer, and he'll then acquire the same feeling about the house. Make the buyer feel that he is the only one who should own this home! Your home is perfect for him and his family.

Be sure to listen to what the potential buyer has to say, and never argue with him. If he says something foolish, just try to ignore it. Never talk down to a buyer; always try to meet him on common ground. If possible, try to strike up a friendship, which will automatically lead to trust and confidence. Try to be patient with a buyer and be sure to avoid high-pressure tactics. Strive to direct him so that he'll make up his own mind in a positive and favorable way. Have all the answers ready and waiting. If he does ask a question you do not have the answer to, be sure you know where the desired information can be ascertained.

Finally, one of the prime precepts of our 'profession' is to "Ask for the order!" Ask him to buy your home and very probably he will.

Let the buyer know you think he should have this home, that the purchase of this home will be in his own best interests, and that you have shown him through your home with the expectation of selling it to him.

If a prospective buyer is interested in purchasing your home, he will normally want to (1) think it over, (2) talk to his lawyer, (3) go over some details, (4) talk to his mommy, or (5) all of the above. You should try to reach an understanding as to exactly when you will be meeting again, and then part as friends.

If you have aroused a positive attitude in the buyer about your home and if it really suits his needs, you very probably have "made the sale," even though he hasn't signed on the dotted line. The biggest part of your battle is over.

11

The Open House

In all the years I've been in real estate, I have never sold an "open house." Very few real estate salesmen have. When we hold an open house, we look upon it primarily as an opportunity to get prospective buyers. It's very rare that a salesman will actually strive to sell the house he is "sitting." Normally, he'll endeavor to get as much information as possible about the prospective buyer — size of family, annual income, area desired, etc. — then go back to his office and check all of the listings currently on the market in order to find the home best suited for this prospective buyer. A real estate salesman knows that the odds are at least 100 to 1 against the buyer actually purchasing the open house and is therefore not going to press the issue. He'll say, "If this house doesn't suit your needs, we have 2,000 others on the market now for you to select from." A statement such as this would not sit well with the seller of the open house, but he's not around to hear it. Generally the seller is very happy with an open house because he feels that the broker is trying very hard to market his home, which, as I have mentioned above, is not necessarily the case.

Probability greatly favors an owner selling his home at an open house over a broker. The reason for this is that the owner's sole purpose is to sell his home, while the broker's primary motive is to attract new clients, which is not in the best interests of the owner.

An Open House is simply an invitation to prospective buyers to stop by and inspect your home. A potential purchaser can merely drop in without the formality of making an appointment for some certain time. Many families like to go for a Sunday drive, have a leisurely lunch, and then see an open house or two. Anyone who knocks on your door must at least like the exterior of the home; otherwise he would have probably kept on driving. In reality, he is half sold at this point, except that the last half is the hardest. An open house attracts a lot of curiosity seekers, but it also brings serious buyers to your door.

Of course, it's best to advertise an open house. But, on the other hand, if a realtor happens to be advertising an open house down the street, you might as well let him pay the advertising bill since the potential buyer probably has to pass by your home on his way either to or from the advertised open house. Just plant your sign, sit back, and reap the benefit at someone elses expense.

As a real estate salesman, I've always contended that a home must be shown as often as possible: the more people who see it, the more likely it's going to sell. You can make effective use of this marketing principle by putting up your "Open House" sign everytime you are home. Yes, I mean Monday, Tuesday, Wednesday, Thursday, Friday, Saturday and Sunday. Look at it this way: You have the opportunity of having seven Sundays in each week. Wouldn't you like to sell your home seven times as fast? Obviously selling a home on your own will somewhat disrupt your normal daily routine, but you should find it a very challenging and a very rewarding experience. Always remember, when you run into a problem not completely covered by this book, just ask your real estate lawyer. He will be able to steer you in the right direction. This experience will instill greater self-confidence in your own ability, widen your horizons, and save you a very heavy broker's commission. If you keep this in mind, you'll find it easy to put up with these slight inconveniences. Remember, put up the "Open House" sign as often as possible and you'll meet the buyer of your home that much sooner!

Most likely someone in real estate will soon mention that you're inviting a burglar everytime you put up an "Open House" sign. In reality, this statement is ludricous and a mere fear tactic. It seems that the real estate profession respects the intelligence of the general public as much as the general public respects the integrity of the real estate salesman. The "scariest" booklet I've seen on this subject is being published by, of all firms, the reowned Chicago Title Insurance Company. The title is (are you ready for this?) "How to Attract Prowlers." I'm sure that the techniques used here have shot down many By Owners because the firm's name lent credence to the intimidating phamphlet. Am I being harsh? Let me quote:

"You'll have all kinds of people prowling everywhere . . . the stories are grizzly . . . what have you got to lose? Without a Realtor, plenty . . . you're fair game for anyone passing by with a few minutes to kill."

Could it be that the reason Chicago Title Insurance Comapny is publishing this booklet is because the greatest proportion of their business comes through the recommendations of the real estate broker? Possibly their motives are far from altruistic. They try to make the seller feel that his home somehow becomes magically burglar-proof when he lists through a broker, which is nonsense. If a burglar wishes to inspect a home in order to determine whether or not to pilfer it, there is no reason he can't do it just as well through a broker. According to the booklet, the broker will screen out the "weirdos." This is ridiculous because there is no method a broker can use to find out whether his client is a thief or burglar. Even if a broker had a form for such a purpose it would be very doubtful that a thief or burglar would "X" the appropriate box.

Open House

We invite you to the Open House at

_____

Date _____ Time _____

If you have a friend or relative who might be interested in purchasing a home in this fine neighborhood, please bring him along. I will be there to tell you all about this outstanding home.

12

The Open-Housing Law

The open-housing law governing the sale of property by real estate brokers was signed by President Johnson in April, 1968 and became fully effective beginning January 1, 1970. Under this law, known as the Civil Rights Act, Title VIII, all housing sold by real estate brokers must comply with the provisions of this legislation. The only exemptions under this act apply to individual owners who sell without the aid of real estate agents and without discriminatory advertising, provided the seller does not own more than three homes or own an apartment building of not more than four units, one of which he occupies. Because of the importance of this law and its provisions, a violation is considered a misdemeanor, punishable by fines up to $1,000 or imprisonment up to one year, with time off for good behavior.

What this legislation means is that if you wish to be a discriminating seller, you have to sell without the aid of a real estate broker. Let's assume you live in a nice clean neighborhood without any bigotry. Everyone presently residing in the area is a nonbigot. Therefore property values are constantly appreciating. The education your children are receiving is of a much higher caliber because all of their classmates are also nonbigots. All the residents in this utopian community realize that their freedom to live together in harmony with their fellow nonbigots is a God-given right and must be protected at all costs.

Now, one dark and dreary night you hear a rapping, rapping at your door. Instinctively you know who it is: they always come on dark and dreary nights. With great deliberation, anxiety, consternation and trepidation, you slowly open the door just ajar — just wide enough so that you can peer out into the fog-laden night — to determine what manner of being is standing in the shadows. One glance is all you need! It's a goddamned bigot! Without a moments hesitation, you slam the door shut, instantly crushing his nose and big toe at the same time.

If you had been working with a broker, you legally could not have done this. You would not have been able to defend yourself against bigotry, which tears at the very fiber of the unity holding our great nation together from sea to shining sea.

13

Can the Buyer Afford Your Home?

It's very uncommon in the sale of real estate for the buyer to pay the entire purchase price in cash. On the contrary, the opposite is much more common; and with the advent of VA financing, the buyer often purchases a home without any down payment at all. Since financing is such an integral part of the vast majority of real estate transactions, it is of the utmost importance for you to find out as soon as possible if your buyer will be able to get a mortgage. Remember, if the buyer cannot financially afford the transaction, then your home should never be taken off the market. When the neighbors see the "For Sale" sign taken down and then replanted a month or two later, they think something is wrong with the house, not with the prospective buyer. This can seriously impair the profitability of the sale in the near future. The longer your home is on the market, the lower your eventual selling price will be.

I have seen many real estate transactions fall by the wayside just prior to closing because the buyers were unable to get proper financing. Usually the reason is that no one ever properly qualified these buyers as to their ability to meet such heavy financial obligations. The one who suffers most is the seller. Quite often, he will have purchased a new home, and be in the process of just moving, only to find out that he now owns two homes and is responsible for the payment of two mortgages. True, the broker is very sorry for his mistake, especially since he lost the commission. It is doubtful though that he will help the seller out of his financial nightmare. Now the broker is going to suggest that he start all over again; but this time, since the seller is in such a tight spot. he'd better lower his asking price so the home will sell fast.

These dire circumstances can be alleviated early in the game if you qualify the buyer as soon as possible. Obviously, you aren't going to try to qualify everyone who wishes to view your home. It would be a waste of time and effort. The time to qualify a buyer is right after you have agreed to the terms of the sale but before he has signed the contract. Ask him to fill out all the information on the "Confidential Buyer Qualification Form." Explain to the buyer that your lawyer needs this form to evaluate the likelihood of whether or not a mortgage will be granted under these specific circumstances. Make it clear that your lawyer doesn't want you to take the home off the market until a fully qualified buyer is found. Most people will gladly fill out a "confidential" form for a lawyer or banker, but they most likely would be reticent

to fill it out for the seller's own personal use. Now, in a very short time you, by yourself or with the aid and advice of your attorney, will be able to determine whether the sale is go or no-go, without tying up your real estate in limbo for 20, 60 or 90 days and all the time wondering what is gnawing at the door to your stomach.

In order to ascertain a buyer's solvency, you have to find out how much he has coming in, how much going out, and how much he has been able to save. By applying the following general credit guidelines to the information obtained with the "Confidential Buyer Qualification Form," you will be readily able to determine the buyer's capabilities.

(1) *Stability of income.* His income for the last three years should be somewhat stable. If he earned $50,000 one year but only $15,000 the other two years, the lending institution will feel that his normal income is only $15,000. Also, it is more favorable if he has been employed at the same firm for the past two years, unless the job change was a promotion.

(2) *Secondary income.* Income from overtime, bonuses, commissions, etc. will be considered normal income if it is of a continuing nature. If secondary income has been steady or constant for the past two years and it is apparent that the income will be sustained in the future, then this income can be added to the basic salary.

(3) *Borrower's credit rating.* If your

prospective buyer has been bankrupt, then for all practical purposes you might as well be blowing against the wind. On the other hand, if he has received a negative credit rating due to circumstances beyond his control (such as an overcharged wife), he may be given favorable consideration.

(4) *Age of borrower.* If the buyer of your home is retired or if he will face forced retirement in the early years of the mortgage, he may have problems in securing financing, unless his pension plus all other sources of income are adequate enough to retire the debt within a reasonable period. The following is a rule of thumb used by many lending institutions: The age of the borrower plus the term of the mortgage should not exceed a total of 80 years. Exceptions to this thumb rule: A man employed at a job that requires physical skill and strength may be old at 45, while a professional man may be considered still in his prime at 55 from the standpoint of occupation age. This can be of great significance because it relates to future earning capacity.

(5) *Outstanding debts.* Hopefully, the borrower doesn't have any long-term outstanding debts that will lower his credit ceiling. Most lenders feel long-term is more than 10 months. If your buyer is paying off a car for the next 11 months, this payment will greatly lower his borrowing capacity. Tell your buyer not to purchase anything and to eat at

McDonald's until the day after closing!

(6) *The self-employed exceptions.* A man who is self-employed is considered by most mortgage houses capable of computing his own ability to repay a loan. It isn't unusual for a businessman to easily repay a loan at the rate of $10,000 a year when he's being taxed on an annual income of only $5,000. He probably could have collected food stamps but decided against it since it might attract IRS ire.

(7) *The actual computation.* Each lending institution will vary somewhat in the way it figures a borrower's credit ceiling. But right now all you're trying to do is to determine the probability of whether or not this buyer is in the ballpark.

Step A: Take his gross monthly salary (before taxes).

Step B: Add all long-term debts together (car, furniture, etc., payments that he will be repaying for at least the next 11 months).

Step C: Subtract the monthly long-term debts from the gross salary.

Step D: Take this answer (the difference) and divide it by 4. The figure you now have is what the buyer can afford to pay monthly for a home including principal, interest, property taxes and home insurance.

Step E: Multiply this monthly mortgage payment (PITI) by 100 and you will have the total approximate mortgage most lenders would give this specific borrower.

Step F: Add the down payment he wishes to make to the total mortgage he is able to get. If this amount is equal to, or greater than, the selling price of your home, everything should be A.O.K. If his mortgage capabilities plus his down payment are less than the selling price of your home, call everything off and be happy you found out right away and not a couple of months down the road.

■ Now, for example:

You're selling your home for $50,000 and the buyer has $10,000 for the down payment. Your buyer's gross monthly salary is $1,400 (Step A).

(Step B)

Car payment	$150
Furniture payment	+50
Total	$200 per month

(Step C)

Gross monthly salary	$1,400
Long-term debts	− 200
	$1,200

(Step D)

$1,200 ÷ 4 = $300

(Step E)

$300 x 100 = $30,000

(Step F)

Maximum mortgage capabilities	$30,000
Down payment	+10,000
	$40,000

■ Conclusion: Your home priced at $50,000 is $10,000 more than he can realistically afford. Don't take the sign down. Tell this (not so) prospective buyer that he will have to get a preliminary mortgage commitment before you will agree to sign a real estate sales contract with him. And in the mean time, your home is still on the market. This way you can have your cake and eat it to!

CONFIDENTIAL BUYER QUALIFICATION FORM

(Please Print)

Name **Carl W. Schulz II**   Age **33**

Spouse **Beverly Schulz**   Age **33**

Address **4303 N. Spaulding**   City **River Grove**   Zip **60012**

Number of Dependents **1**   Ages **9 + 6**   Ph { Home **823-1161** Office **389-5934**

Financing Desired: VA ☐   FHA ☐   CONV. ☒   OTHER _____

Preferred Down Payment $ **10,000**   Maximum, if needed $ **same**

Preferred Monthly Payment $ **300**   Maximum, if needed $ **350**

Husband

Employer **Pierce International**

Address **211 E Touhy, Des Plaines**

Position **Manger**   How Long **8** yrs.

Average Monthly Income $ **1,000**

Wife

Employer **Tiara Salon of Beauty**

Address **127 S. N.W. Hwy, Park Ridge**

Position **Beautician**   How Long **3** yrs.

Average Monthly Income $ **400**

Total Earnings before taxes for last three years:

19 **73** $ **16,784**   19 **74** $ **16,490**   19 **75** $ **17,048**

	Monthly	Yearly
Husband's Income	$ **800**	$ **9,600**
Other Income (explain) **Bonus**	$ **200**	$ **2,400**
Wife's Income	$ **300**	$ **3,600**
Other Income (explain) **Commission**	$ **100**	$ **1,200**
Totals	$ **1,400**	$ **16,800**

Assets		Liabilities	Monthly Payment	Unpaid Balance
Cash	$ **2,000**	Auto	$ **150**	$ **2,100**
Stocks, Bonds, etc.	$ **8,000**	Real Estate	$ **—**	$ **—**
Life Insurance (Cash Value)	$ **950**	Loans	$ **50**	$ **950**
Real Estate	$ **—**	Other	$ **—**	$ **—**
Other	$ **4,500**	Other	$ **—**	$ **—**
Total	$ **15,350**	Total	$ **200**	$ **3,050**

Have you ever been involved in a Bankruptcy, Wage Garnishment, Mortgage Foreclosure, Receivership, or Judgement proceedings, or any other credit problems during the past ten years? ☐ Yes ☒ No   If yes, please explain on the reverse side.

I hereby certify that the foregoing information is true and accurate to the best of my knowledge and belief.

Date **May 24, 1976**   *Carl W. Schulz II*

Signature of Buyer

14

The Contract is Simple, but the Words Aren't !

Interpreting a contract is much like interpreting the Bible: it's always best to have God on your side. With that though in mind, the purpose of this chapter is to explain in layman's terms what a real estate sales contract is and what some of the possible contingencies are. But it would be ludicrous to suggest that this book could completely replace the advice of a real estate lawyer. While I can only highlight problem areas in contract law, a real estate attorney can offer specific solutions to these problems.

Essentially, a contract for the sale of real estate is an agreement between a seller and buyer in which all of the terms of the transaction are explicitly set fourth. It gives an exact description of the property, the terms of the sale, the price, the place and time of closing, and the date of possession.

It is not uncommon for circumstances to necessitate the inclusion of other contract clauses to cover special situations or contingencies. The most common contingency is a contract contingent upon the buyer being able to get a loan on acceptable terms. If the buyer is unable to get a mortgage or if the terms of the mortgage would be unacceptable, then this contingency would effectively void the contract. Usually, if a contingency cannot be fulfilled, the contract can be deemed void (depending on the specific wording of the contingency). Therefore, contingencies are normally the loophole through which a buyer can wiggle his way out of the contract.

There is no such animal as a standard contract for the sale of real estate. The following contract we have reproduced represents a typical form used in many areas of the United States. Undoubtedly, the "standard" contract used in your locale varies somewhat from this form, but the content should be essentially the same. Whether you use this contract or your lawyer draws up his own contract is purely a matter of preference. If your lawyer favors one form over another, always abide by his wishes.

■ Let's examine the component parts of the specimen contract we have included. Each of the following explanatory paragraphs are preceeded by a number corresponding to a like number-keyed section on the specimen contract — e.g., paragraph (1) below refers to section (1) in the contract.

(1)   "Date . . ." This is the date that the contract is to be presented for acceptance.

(2)   ". . . OWNERS . . ." Be sure to use the full legal names in identifying all owners.

(3)   ". . . known as . . ." The majority of states do not require a full legal description of the property to be included in the contract; you are required to include a description that will clearly establish the identity and location of the property involved.

(4)   "Lot . . ." Check your survey to find the dimensions of the lot. If this is not readily available, then physically measure the length and width. Try to be very accurate, a varience of five feet can void the contract: the buyer could state that he's not getting all he bargained for.

". . . improvements . . ." This is a list of attached improvements usually included in the sale of residential real estate. The important phrase in this section is "if any." This means that if some of the items listed are not presently in the home, they therefore are not included in the sale because they don't exist. You can't sell something you don't have. IMPORTANT: If your water softner is rented and not owned CROSS IT OFF THE LIST; otherwise you'll probably have to purchase a water softner for the new owners because it's presently on the premises.

(5)   ". . . RIDER(S) . . ." Since the vast majority of contracts have riders or contingencies attached to them, we have included this statement making specific reference to this fact. IMPORTANT: If your contract is the exception, if there

are no contingencies or riders attached, **CROSS OUT THIS PARAGRAPH.**

(6) "...price..." This is the total price the buyer is going to pay the seller.

(7) "Deposit..." This is the amount of money the purchaser hands the seller at the time he presents this contract.

"...deposited with..." Normally, the deposit will be held in escrow by your attorney.

(8) "...to be increased..." You should require a 10 per cent deposit from your buyer. It just shows that he is sincere and earnest. He may not have the full 10 per cent at the time he signs the contract, and you may therefore have to accept whatever he now has. Give him 5 to 10 days to increase the deposit to a full 10 per cent. **IMPORTANT:** If the initial earnest deposit is a full 10 per cent, then **CROSS OUT** everything from "to be increased" to "acceptance hereof."

(9) "...if not accepted by..." Normally, you should write in "upon presentation" if at all possible. That way he has to decide then and there. If you let the buyer sleep on it, he may have a nightmare. If his wife isn't there or if he wants his lawyer to review the contract, then write in a specific time and date — *as soon as possible!* Also, you can get around this situation by having him sign the contract contingent on the approval

of his wife or lawyer (see the discussion of riders later in this chapter).

(10) "Cash to be paid..." Add the initial 10 per cent deposit to the amount of the mortgage loan he is going to need. Then deduct this amount from the total purchase. The difference is the cash he will need at the closing.

Example: Assume the total purchase price is $50,000, the deposit is $5,000 and the buyers mortgage loan is $40,000. Compute the cash to be paid at closing as follows:

Initial 10% deposit	$ 5,000
Mortgage loan	+40,000
Total	$45,000
Purchase price	$50,000
Deduct	−45,000
Cash needed at closing	$ 5,000

(11) "Balance to be paid..." In the vast majority of real estate sales, the buyer needs to finance a portion of the purchase price. Therefore, we have included this mortgage contingency in the contract. **IMPORTANT:** If your buyer is the exception because he is going to pay the full purchase price in cash, then **CROSS OUT** this whole section from "Balance to be..." to "...SHALL BE VOID."

(12) ". . . within_____days . . ." This varies from area to area, but usually on a conventional mortgage 14 days should be sufficient time for the buyer to get a commitment. On a VA or FHA loan, 30 days may be necessary.

(13) ". . . mortgage loan of . . ." This is the total amount of financing the buyer is going to need.

". . . not to exceed . . ." Fill in the current interest rate, taking into consideration the amount of financing he needs in relation to his down payment. The interest rates are higher on 90 per cent loans than they are on 80 per cent loans. Your local banker will be happy to inform you about the current mortgage-loan interest rates.

(14) ". . . period of . . ." As a rule of thumb, fill in 25 years. It is not uncommon for lending institutions to give a maximum loan life of 25 years, so if he is trying to get a 30-or-40-year mortgage at these institutions, it can void the contract.

(15) "IN THE EVENT . . ." If the buyer is unable to get a loan commitment and he fails to notify you, then he is liable for the purchase of your home without a mortgage. If he does notify you of his inability to get a loan within the specified number of days, then you have to return his deposit.

(16) ". . . or at . . ." Quite often the closing is also held at the purchaser's attorney's office.

(17) ". . . on . . ." This varies from area to area and should be verified with your real estate attorney: 45 to 60 days after the signing of this contract is common (make sure this date doesn't fall on a weekend or holiday).

(18) "Title to be . . ." When title to real estate is being conveyed, it is presumed that it is being conveyed free and clear of all encumberances or claims, except for those expressly stated. The prime function of this section is to state the nature of any claims that may affect the title to the property. It lists any conditions that limit or govern the use of the title being conveyed. Fill in the year in which the closing will take place: "for 19____ ." If no leases are to be assigned, CROSS OUT "existing leases as follows (to be assigned to Buyer)."

(19) "The following items . . ." This section provides for the sharing of the costs of certain items between the buyer and seller so that each one bears his fair share, the seller paying for the period in which he owned the property, the buyer paying the balance.

(20) "At or before closing . . ." The purpose of this section is to give the seller sufficient time to bring down good title. If the title is found to be defective, the seller has an extra 30 days to cure the defect. If he is unable to do so, then the contract can become null and void at the

discretion of the buyer.

(21) "Date of possession . . ." This date varies from area to area. Sometimes it is the same as the date of closing, while other times it can be a day, or a couple days, after closing for the sake of convenience. It is difficult to be at a closing and move furniture at the same time.

(22) "Earnest money . . ." Normally, the buyer's deposit is held in escrow by the seller's attorney, as stated above. This clause covers the distribution of these monies if either the buyer or seller default on the contract. If the buyer defaults, the deposit is paid to the seller as damages. If the seller defaults, the deposit has to be returned and the seller can still be bound by the contract.

(23) "If prior to closing . . ." This clause states that the seller is responsible for maintaining fire insurance until the date of possession; and if the residence is "destroyed or materially damaged by fire," the contract can become null and void at the option of the buyer.

The remainder of the contract is self-explanatory.

CONTRACT TO PURCHASE REAL ESTATE

(1)   Date Presented_____

(2) **TO THE LEGAL OWNERS:**_____

(3) I (We) offer to purchase the property known as: (The parties hereto reserve the right to insert the legal description at a later date.)

_____County of_____State of_____

(4) Lot approximately_____, together with improvements thereon including the following, if any, now on premises: water softner; storm windows and doors; screens; shades; venetian blinds; drapery rods; radiator covers; T.V. antenna; heating; lighting and plumbing fixtures; central cooling; ventilating and air purifying system; awnings; attached mirrors, shelving, cabinets and bookcases; planted vegetation; and all fixtures and fittings appurtenant to or used in the operation of the premises, on the following terms:

(5) This contract to purchase is subject to the terms and conditions of the RIDER(S) attached hereto which is incorporated in and made a part of this contract by reference.

(6) Total purchase price $_____Dollars, payable as follows:

(7) Deposit — Initial earnest money $_____deposited with _____

(8) to be increased to 10% of the purchase price within_____days after acceptance hereof.

(9) Said deposit money shall be returned and this offer shall be void if not accepted by (date and time; or upon presentation)_____

(10) Cash to be paid on delivery of deed $_____

(11) Balance to be paid as follows: The parties hereto understand that it is necessary for the Purchaser to have

(12) had made available to him within_____days after the date of acceptance hereof by the Seller, a

(13) commitment for a mortgage loan of $_____with interest not to exceed_____% per

(14) annum, over a period of_____years, at the reasonable and usual loan commission. Seller shall allow inspections of the premises and furnish any pertinent information required by Purchaser's lending institution in reference to making the loan commitment. If, after the Purchaser has made every reasonable effort to procure such commitment and has been unable to do so, the Purchaser shall serve written notice thereof upon the Seller within the time specified herein for procuring said commitment for a loan, this contract shall thereupon become null and void and all monies paid by Purchaser shall be refunded to him.

(15) IN THE EVENT PURCHASER DOES NOT SERVE WRITTEN NOTICE OF HIS FAILURE TO PROCURE A LOAN COMMITMENT UPON THE SELLER WITHIN THE NUMBER OF DAYS AS HEREIN PROVIDED, THEN THIS CONTRACT SHALL CONTINUE IN FULL FORCE AND EFFECT AND THIS PARAGRAPH SHALL BE VOID.

(16) The title closing or escrow pay out shall be at Purchaser's lending institution or at_____

(17) _____ on _____
or before, providing title has been shown good or accepted by Purchaser by conveyance by stamped warranty deed and payment of purchase price.

(18) Title to be conveyed subject to: General real estate taxes for 19____and subsequent years; building, building line and use or occupancy restrictions, conditions or covenants of record; easements and party wall agreements; installments of special assessments falling due after title has been conveyed; special assessments for improvements not yet completed; zoning and building laws or ordinances; roads and highways, if any; existing leases as follows (to be assigned to Buyer)_____

(19) The following items are to be prorated to date of possession: General real estate taxes (based on most recent ascertainable taxes); interest on encumberences; electric light and gas; water taxes; rents; janitor (including vacation allowance); fuel at market price; and any other usual proratable items.

(20) At or before closing Seller shall furnish to Purchaser one of the following items covering date hereof showing marketable title in Grantor (Seller): (1) A merchantable abstract of title brought down to date hereof, (2) Commitment for title insurance issued by any title insurance company licensed to do business in the state in which the above described property is located, brought down to date hereof, (3) A Torrens certificate accompanied by a Torrens title tax search. If the evidence of title discloses defects Seller shall have 30 additional days from date evidence of title is furnished to cure such defects and notify Purchaser. If Seller is unable to cure such defects Purchaser may, at his election, terminate this contract, or Purchaser may take the title as it then is (with the right to deduct from the purchase price the ascertainable amounts of liens or encumberances) by notifying Seller and tendering performance.

(21) Date of possession by Purchaser shall be not later than 12:00 noon (Date)_____ providing sale has been closed.

(22) Earnest money and this contract shall be held in escrow by_____ for the benefit of the parties hereto. If Purchaser defaults, earnest money shall be forfeited and paid to Seller. At Seller's election such forfeiture may be in full settlement of all damages. If Seller defaults, earnest money, at option of Purchaser, shall be refunded to Purchaser, but such refunding shall not release Seller from the obligation of this contract.

(23) If prior to closing, improvements on said premises shall be destroyed or materially damaged by fire or any other casualty, this contract at the option of Purchaser shall become null and void.

Existing mortgage and other lien indebtedness may be paid at closing out of sale proceeds.

Prior to closing, Seller will furnish an acceptable survey by a licensed land serveyor showing the location of the buildings thereon to be within the lot lines and showing no encroachments of improvements from adjoining properties.

Purchaser may place a mortgage on this property and apply proceeds on purchase.

This contract to purchase when signed by Purchaser(s) and Seller(s) constitutes a binding contract.

Seller warrants to Purchaser that no notice from any city, village or other governmental authority of any dwelling code violation has heretofore been issued and received by the owner or his agent with respect to any dwelling structure on said real estate.

PURCHASER_____ Address_____

PURCHASER_____ _____

This_____day of_____ 19___, we accept this offer to perform and convey or cause to be conveyed according to the terms of this contract.

SELLER _____ Address_____

SELLER _____ _____

If your attorney decides that the foregoing contract is satisfactory, then you will be able to sit down with your buyer and explain it to him by referring to the specific keyed paragraphs in this chapter, thereby facilitating the closing of the deal while the buyer is still hot. This can expedite the sale of your home because most residences are sold on weekends, when most lawyers are flying to the Ozarks. Invariably, they are unavailable at the time the contracts should be signed. If your attorney has previously gone over the contractural rough spots with you, then it shouldn't be necessary for him to be on hand at the signing of the contract. You should be able to fall back on this book at that time. However, if you feel uneasy about some strange contingency that the buyer wishes to insert, hold your horses until you can get the advice of your learned counsel.

RIDERS

■ The definition of a rider is any addition to a document or contract. Quite often, circumstances necessitate the inclusion of additional contract clauses to cover special circumstances or contingent conditions. These riders can be typed or handwritten. They must be securely stapled to the main body of the contract and signed by both the buyer and seller. The most common riders are as follows:

PERSONAL PROPERTY RIDER

RE: Property at _____

It is understood and agreed between the SELLERS and the PURCHASERS of the aforementioned property that the following items, presently on the premises and in use, are to be included in the purchase price of $_____   _____

_____

_____

_____

_____

_____

_____

_____

_____

_____

_____

_____

Date _____ Purchaser _____

Purchaser _____

Date _____ Seller _____

Seller _____

■ The following rider is somewhat complicated, and its ramifications should be reviewed with your attorney. Let's assume that the buyer of your home already owns a home that he is presently trying to sell. He wants to buy your home but is worried that his present residence won't sell and that he could possibly end up owning two homes. The solution to his problem is to buy your home contingent on his home selling on or before a certain agreed upon date. The only problem here is that if his home doesn't sell, you're up the creek without a paddle.

Now here is your paddle. The solution to your problem is to insert a contingency in his contingency (you're falling asleep – I can tell) stating that if you get another offer on your home that is better than his offer (not contingent on the sale of a home), then you'll give him 24 hours to remove his contingency: otherwise, you'll accept the second offer. This rider can be very beneficial to you because you have a potentially strong buyer and at the same time your home is kept on the market while the contingency is effective. Keep your "For Sale" sign up until your home is 100 per cent SOLD!

CONTRACT CONTINGENT ON THE SALE OF BUYER'S PRESENT HOME

THIS RIDER IS ATTACHED TO AND MADE PART OF THE REAL ESTATE SALES CONTRACT

DATED: _____, 19____between _____ and

_____, as Purchasers, and _____ and

_____, as Sellers.

This contract to purchase is subject to the sale of the Buyer's present home located at:_____

_____County_____State_____

on or before (date)_____ 19____.

If said property is not sold within the time specified the Buyer shall give the Seller or his agent written notice as provided herein of such failure within the time allowed for the sale whereupon this contract shall become null and void and all monies paid by the Buyer shall be refunded. In the event the Buyer does not serve notice upon the Seller or his agent as herein provided then this contract shall continue in full force and effect and this condition shall be void.

Seller shall have the right to cancel this contract by giving the Buyer herein 24 hours written notice that the Seller has received a bonafide contract to purchase the property herein non-contingent on the sale of other real estate, on like or better terms than those set forth herein, if within said 24 hour period Buyer does not delete this contingency in writing thereby agreeing to complete this purchase regardless of whether or not Buyer's home is sold. If not so removed, this contract shall become null and void and all monies paid by Buyer shall be refunded.

Date_____

Accepted:

Purchaser _____

Purchaser _____

Seller _____

Seller _____

■ By the use of the following rider, you can sell your home to either the husband or wife contingent on the spouse's approval.

CONTRACT CONTINGENT ON SPOUSE'S APPROVAL

THIS RIDER IS ATTACHED TO AND MADE PART OF THE REAL ESTATE SALES CONTRACT

DATED: _____, 19____, between _____and

_____, as Purchasers, and_____ and

_____, as Sellers.

This contract to purchase is subject to the approval of the property by Buyer's spouse within (max. 48 hours)_____hours of (date of contract)_____time (of contract)_____a.m./p.m. o'clock. In the event the spouse does not approve of the property, written notice as provided herein shall be given to the Seller or his agent within the time specified for said spouse's approval and thereupon this contract shall become null and void and all monies paid by the Buyer shall be refunded to him. In the event the Buyer does not serve said notice upon Seller or his agent that the Buyer's spouse does not approve of said property then this contract shall continue in full force and effect and this condition shall be void.

Date_____

Accepted:

Purchaser _____

Purchaser _____

Seller _____

Seller _____

■ The following rider is a VA appraisal contingency that has to be attached to every contract in which the purchaser is applying for a VA mortgage. This rider states that if the appraisal of the home doesn't equal the amount of the mortgage requested, then the buyer, at his option, has to be refunded his deposit and the contract is null and void.

VA APPRAISAL CONTINGENCY

THIS RIDER IS ATTACHED TO AND MADE PART OF THE REAL ESTATE SALES CONTRACT

DATED: _____ , 19 ____ , between _____ and

_____ , as Purchasers, and _____ and

_____ , as Sellers.

AMENDMENT TO VA CONTRACT

"It is expressly agreed that, notwithstanding any other provision of this contract, the Purchaser shall not incur any penalty by forfeiture of earnest money or otherwise or be obligated to complete the purchase of the property described herein, if the contract purchase price or cost exceeds the reasonable value of the property established by the Veterans Administration. The Purchaser shall, however, have the privilege and option of proceeding with the consummation of this contract without regard to the amount of the reasonable value established by the Veterans Administration."

Date _____

Veteran Purchaser _____

Purchaser _____

Seller _____

Seller _____

■ The following rider is an FHA appraisal contingency that has to be attached to every contract in which the purchaser is applying for a FHA mortgage. This rider states that if the appraisal of the home doesn't equal the amount of the mortgage requested, then the buyer, at his option, has to be refunded his deposit and the contract is null and void.

FHA APPRAISAL CONTINGENCY

THIS RIDER IS ATTACHED TO AND MADE PART OF THE REAL ESTATE SALES CONTRACT

DATED: _____ , 19___, between _____ and

_____ , as Purchasers, and _____ and

_____ , as Sellers.

"It is expressly agreed that, notwithstanding any other provisions of this contract, the purchaser shall not be obligated to complete the purchase of the property described herein or to incur any penalty by forfeiture of earnest money deposits or otherwise unless the seller has delivered to the purchaser a written statement issued by the Federal Housing Commissioner setting forth the appraised value of the property for mortgage insurance purposes of not less than $_____ , which statement the seller hereby agrees to deliver to the purchaser promptly after such appraised value statement is made available to the seller."

"The purchaser shall, however, have the privilege and option of proceeding with the consummation of this contract without regard to the amount of the appraised valuation made by the Federal Housing Commissioner."

Date _____ Purchaser _____

Purchaser _____

Date _____ Seller _____

Seller _____

■ The following two riders are both contingent on attorney's approval. The first refers to the buyer's attorney's approval. Note the words "as it pertains to legal matters only." This phrase is not included in the rider for the seller's attorney's approval. Your attorney therefore would have the right to not approve the contract for reasons other than mere legal form. The buyer's attorney would be able to disapprove on grounds "as it pertains to legal matters only."

CONTRACT CONTINGENT ON BUYER'S ATTORNEY'S APPROVAL

THIS RIDER IS ATTACHED TO AND MADE PART OF THE REAL ESTATE SALES CONTRACT

DATED:_____, 19___, between _____and

_____, as Purchasers, and _____and

_____, as Sellers.

This contract to purchase is subject to the approval of the Buyer's attorney as it pertains to legal matters only, with (max. 48 hours)_____hours of (date of contract)_____time (of contract)_____a.m./p.m. o'clock. In the absence of written notice within the time specified herein, this provision shall be deemed waived by all parties hereto and this contract shall be in full force and effect.

Date _____

Accepted:

Purchaser _____

Purchaser _____

Seller _____

Seller _____

CONTRACT CONTINGENT ON
SELLER'S ATTORNEY'S APPROVAL

THIS RIDER IS ATTACHED TO AND MADE PART OF THE REAL ESTATE SALES CONTRACT

DATED: _____ , 19___, between _____ and

_____ , as Purchasers, and _____ and

_____ , as Sellers.

This contract to purchase is subject to the approval of the Seller's attorney within (max. 48 hours)_____hours of (date of contract)_____time (of contract)_____a.m./p.m. o'clock. In the absence of written notice within the time specified herein, this provision shall be deemed waived by all parties hereto and this contract shall be in full force and effect.

Date _____

Accepted:

Purchaser _____

Purchaser _____

Seller _____

Seller _____

■ In conclusion, if your contract has any contingency attached to it, then your house isn't completely sold. And until that contingency has been removed, continue showing your home to other prospective buyers. It is not necessary for you to divulge to these prospects that you already have a contingent offer. When they present an offer, just tell them you'll need 24 hours (or whatever length of time the contingency is for) in which to decide whether or not you will accept or reject their offer.

Rule of thumb: Keep your "Home For Sale By Owner" sign planted as long as possible!

HOME TEAM | 7 POINTS
VISITORS | 3 POINTS

15

What are Points?

If the purchaser of your home is acquiring his mortgage under a VA or FHA loan, you will be notified that you have to pay a certain number of points. Points are an important cost factor in the majority of real estate transactions today, yet most people do not understand what they mean or how to legally get around them.

Whether they are called "points," "loan brokerage fees," "discounts," or "new loan fees," they all mean the same. Points provide the basic ingredient behind over 50 per cent of all home sales in the United States. Without points, home sales with low down payments would not be possible. Since points are a very important part of today's residential market, an understanding of what they mean is vital.

Through the use of points, extra money can be charged by the lending institution so that they will be able to profitably make loans on residences under present-day money-market conditions. Points automatically increase the profit or rate of return to the lender.

It is very easy to figure points. One point is 1 per cent of the amount of the loan. So if five points are being charged on a loan of $40,000 just multiply 5% x $40,000 which equals $2,000, a fairly sizable amount of money, especially if it is coming out of your pocket. Note that the points are figured on the amount of the loan, not the selling price of the property.

Most likely you're wondering why points are necessary on VA and FHA loans. In order to create a condition whereby the majority of the people can buy their own home, the U.S. government establishes a maximum rate ceiling that a borrower may be charged on any government-insured loan (either FHA or VA). This rate is always lower than the conventional mortgage rates. Also, it is important to realize that the federal government does not loan the money: it insures that the loan will be repaid to the lender. If the borrower defaults, the government will repay the balance of the loan to the lending institution. The problem is that the interest rate ceiling established by the federal government is not high enough to attract money from the various lending institutions. There are many other areas where they can invest their capital and receive a rate of return that will exceed that obtainable from FHA and VA loans

— e.g., stocks, bonds, conventional loans, etc. In order to make these government-insured loans sufficiently attractive in order to compete with the various other forms of investments, the idea of paying points came into being. Actually, points make it possible for a lender to make FHA and VA loans.

The required number of points will vary from time to time as the cost of borrowing money fluctuates, depending on the laws of supply and demand in the money markets. As money becomes scarce, the points go up; and conversely, when the volume of available money increases, the points go down. But during these point fluctuations, the government's fixed rate of interest on VA and FHA loans remains unchanged.

Why do you the seller have to pay the points on the buyers mortgage? Simply because the federal government regulations on VA and FHA loans do not allow the purchaser to pay points. It's important to remember that if the government makes a rule or regulation, it's not necessary for it to make sense. But by paying the prevailing points, you make it possible for your residence to be sold through government-insured financing. The vast majority of home buyers in the lower and medium price range obtain FHA or VA loans. The low interest rate coupled with both the low down payment and the long-term loan result in lower monthly payments, which enable many people to buy homes that they could not afford otherwise. These FHA and VA loans bring many more buyers into the home market and therefore greatly improve chances for a property owner to make a sale.

I will now illustrate how you can get away from actually paying the points without the government being wiser. Sound illegal? It's not! Hardly a day goes by when I don't see a residential transaction in which the buyer in reality paid the points.

Let's first create a hypothetical case in which your appraiser has determined the house should sell for $39,000 and you are asking $40,000. You have two prospective buyers who have just simultaneously presented offers to purchase your home. Mr. Smith is offering $38,000 and will get a conventional mortgage, while Mr. Jones is offering the full price of $40,000 but is planning on getting 100 per cent VA mortgage with the points presently at 5 (or $2,000). It doesn't matter which offer you accept since either way your net will be exactly the same. What you should do is reject both offers or counter one of the offers for $1,000 more. Which means you can tell Mr. Jones that you won't sell your home to him for less than $41,000, or $1,000 more than your asking price! In this way, you have actually made the purchaser pay the points. Always remember that you never have to accept an offer that doesn't net you what you require.

16

Help Your Buyer Get Financing !

Financing the purchase of a home is quite often the most cumbersome step in the whole selling procedure. It is very probable that you will have a ready, willing and able buyer who can't get a mortgage. To help alleviate this problem, it's a good idea for you to have a basic knowledge of the kinds of mortgages that are available as well as have a source of mortgage money where your buyer can go.

A real estate mortgage is defined as the pledging of property as security for the repayment of a loan.

Basically, there are three catagories for residential mortgage money. The first one we are going to deal with is the Federal Housing Administration (FHA), which came into being during the Depression in 1934. It was established to facilitate the granting of mortgage money by lending institutions, based upon a government guarantee to take over the mortgage in case of default. In actuality, the FHA guarantee backs the credit of the homeowner with the credit of the federal government. Through the effectiveness of this program and its general public acceptance, it has caused the standardization of the practices of the lending institutions and has also upgraded the quality of construction in the home-building industry.

Under Federal Housing Administration regulations, the guaranteed loans may be made only through approved lending institutions, which further protects the borrower from unethical practices or exorbitant rates. The regulations also provide for uniform appraisals, standardized loan applications, and guidelines to be met by the borrower — *e.g.,* good credit rating, a steady income sufficient enough to make the monthly loan payments without straining the family budget, etc.

The interest rate charged for FHA insured mortgages varies with the general conditions in the money market, but it's always competitive: normally a half of a per cent less than a conventional mortgage with a down payment that is always much less. The monthly payment is computed on the prevailing interest rate at the time of closing, not when the borrower applies for the loan from the mortgagee. Sometimes the lending institution will "guarantee" the prevailing rate at the time of the application, but usually the borrower will have to ask. Many lending institutions will bend on this point if they are requested by the borrower to guarantee the prevailing interest rate.

The FHA mortgage is an excellent means whereby a potential home buyer without a large down payment can buy a home and still be somewhat assured that he is not being taken advantage of by an unscrupulous builder or lender.

You or your prospective buyer can obtain up-to-the-minute information on FHA rules, regulations, prevailing interest rates, and other costs from a local approved bank, savings and loan association or lending institution. Or write to the U.S. Department of Housing and Urban Development (HUD), 451 7th Street S.W., Washington, D.C. 20410.

The second form of residential financing we are going to cover is the VA mortgage, which dates back to the early 1940s. As World War II came to a close, it became increasingly apparent to Congress that legislation was needed to assist returning war veterans in readjusting to private life. Thus, in 1944 the Serviceman's Readjustment Act, commonly referred to as the GI Bill of Rights was enacted by the congressional leaders of a country grateful to those who had honorably served in its armed forces.

The GI Bill of Rights contained several government-loan-guaranty and monetary-contribution programs for the returning veteran. The Veterans Administration was authorized to partially guarantee loans made to qualified veterans by approved lending institutions. The Veterans Administration, unlike FHA, can make direct loans in areas where other money is not available. For example, from time to time the Veterans Administration has allocated sums of money for various counties to be loaned to veterans who have been unable to obtain a VA loan from a bank or other lending institution. If the veteran has been refused at two lending institutions, he can apply directly to the Veterans Administration for his mortgage.

Since the end of World War II, more than seven million veterans have bought homes with the aid of VA (GI) loans. The program has been amended from time to time to allow for changes in interest rates and to increase the amount of the guaranty. The last amendment was signed into law in 1974 and was titled the Veterans Housing Act of 1974. The important parts of this act are as follows:

(1) As of January 2, 1975, the maximum guaranty for a loan to finance the purchase of a home is 60 per cent of the loan amount, or $17,500 whichever is less. There are no actual limits placed on the amount of the mortgage loan that can be made to a veteran and still be guaranteed. However, the guaranty limits constitute a built-in maximum. For example, a VA-guaranteed home loan of $70,000 with no down payment is equivilant to a conventional loan of 75 per cent with 25 per cent down, since $17,500 is being guaranteed by the government. It would not be prudent for a lending institution to make a VA loan over $70,000 because the risk factor would be increased beyond normal practices. Thus, a VA mortgage loan ceiling is created at $70,000 as long as the guaranty is at $17,500.

(2) No down payment is required by the VA. However, in the event the veteran agrees to purchase the home for a price in excess of the appraised value as determined by the Veterans Administration, the veteran is required to pay cash for the total amount over the appraised value.

(3) Closing costs may not be included in the loan and must be paid in cash at the time of closing. Also, closing costs may not be greater than listed in the VA schedule of permissible charges applicable to loans for the purchase of a residence.

(4) The maximum term of the loan is 30 years.

(5) There is no prepayment penalty.

(6) The monthly mortgage payments must include principal, interest, real estate taxes and fire insurance (PITI).

(7) The veteran must certify that he plans to live at the residence he is purchasing. However, in the event that the veteran moves to another home at a later date, he may rent out the home that was financed by a VA loan.

(8) And lastly, a VA mortgage can be taken over or assumed by another purchaser, who need not be a veteran. It's not necessary to get the approval of the VA or the lending institution.

If you wish further information, the VA publishes two informative booklets: "Questions and Answers on Guaranteed Loans for Veterans" and "To The Home-Buying Veteran." These booklets can be acquired by writing to the

Veterans Administration, Washington, D.C. 20420.

The third method of financing is the conventional mortgage obtained from a bank, savings and loan association or other lending institution, which does not rely on guarantees from any governmental agency but does rely on the credit and reputation of the borrower and the appreciation of the value of the property on which the loan is made. These lending institutions consider the single-family residence a major source of their investment business. When the prospective buyer of your home is looking for a loan, he should approach his own bank or the lending institution that is presently holding your mortgage. Even if they cannot make the loan because the home is out of their "area" or because of a shortage of funds, etc., the loan officer will normally recommend a lender that can be of assistance.

If there is a prepayment penalty in the mortgage you now have, it is not uncommon for the mortgage house to waive this charge if the buyer of your residence applies for his mortgage through the same lender. This can be a substantial savings to you and is worthwhile

checking into.

In general, the down payment on the conventional mortgage is higher than either the FHA or VA mortgages: usually 20 to 25 per cent is required. Since the conventional mortgage market responds to the fluctuations in interest rates much more rapidly than both the FHA and VA, the overall availability of conventional mortgage money is normally much greater. Conventional mortgages account for over 60 per cent of all home loans made.

Another form of the conventional mortgage is the "purchase-money mortgage." This mortgage is a loan given by the seller to the purchaser for all or part of the selling price of the home. This is an alternative means of financing between two individuals, that excludes the lending institution. It can also be used to enable a home buyer to purchase the property when he has less down payment than required by a financial institution. If you have a sound buyer who hasn't saved enough for the full down payment, discuss the possibility of a purchase-money mortgage with your real estate attorney. It may be just what the doctor ordered.

the Loan-a-Ranger to the rescue!

17

What is Title Insurance?

As the ownership of real estate became more valuable, it became increasingly important to provide safeguards to protect the true owner from loss of title through error, claim or fraud.

When you purchase stock in a corporation, you don't have to know if the stock broker is married, divorced or single. If you buy a television set, you don't have to know if the salesman has a past-due tax bill. When you buy a car, you don't have to worry if the dealer has an illegitimate offspring.

But when you purchase real estate, all of these things become extremely vital. You must have a complete investigation made to prove that the property you purchased is actually yours.

Since the beginning of time, real estate has always been considered the most important material possession a man can have. Its importance and value are evidenced by the multitude of laws that have been enacted for its protection. As a result of these strong safeguards, the owner or real estate, or title holder, has certain rights that he can pass on to his family and heirs or dispose of as he so desires.

It is also possible for others to have a right in the property. If there is a mortgage, the lending institution has a right until the loan is paid. If the property is being rented, the tenant has the right to occupy until the end of the lease. If the real estate taxes are not paid, the local government has the right to sell the property to pay these debts. There are many rights that can make someone a part owner in the real estate. Normally, the part owner cannot be deprived of his interest until the claim is settled. Even if the original owner sells the real estate without his knowledge, the part owner's claim is still good against the new owner.

Therefore, when real estate is purchased, the only sure way to be confident that the title is clear and full rights of ownership are being passed on is to be positive that all previous claims have been satisfied.

The deed a purchaser receives at the time of closing doesn't necessarily give him clear title. Actually, all it does is transfer the sellers right of ownership. If the seller does not in reality own the property, the buyer has no right to the property whatsoever. Outstanding claims and rights cannot be determined from the deed.

The history of the ownership of a parcel of land going back as long as records were kept is called the "chain of title." This continuous record of all the changes in ownership that took place is like a chain, with each transaction serving as a link. And as with any chain, it's only as strong as the weakest link. If any link in the chain is defective, title will be defective from that point on.

Needless to say, it's of the greatest importance for the purchaser of a home to get clear title. But this means that he must have knowledge of any and all claims against the property so that he can be certain that they're cleared before the time of closing. It also means that he must be protected against any unknown or undiscovered claims that might arise sometime in the future and thereby threaten his title and possession of the home. The purpose of title insurance is to provide this twofold type of protection.

The method by which the title-insurance companies learn of any claims against the property is through a thorough search of the public records. This is the first step they take in order to insure good title. They track down every entry on all the public records that might possibly affect the title of the real estate.

The title-insurance company then makes out a report on all the defects its investigations uncovered so that these matters can be corrected and cleared up as soon as possible. This is the first benefit a home buyer receives from title insurance.

It's very possible that there are defects in the title that don't show up on the public records. This can and does happen. They are called "hidden risks" — any undiscovered claims against a parcel of real estate that possibly will not come to light until long after the time of purchase. The protection of the homeowner against a loss from a claim that can't be discovered by a thorough examination of the public records is the second benefit provided by title insurance.

The title to the home the buyer has paid for and for which he has received a deed can be seriously threatened or even completely lost by such circumstances as unpaid back taxes, forgery, judgments against the property, errors in the public records, or that illegitimate offspring we mentioned previously. A homeowner has to protect himself against these bastards.

Unlike most other forms of insurance, the original premium is the buyer's only cost as long as he or his heirs own the real estate. There are no annual payments to keep the owner's title-insurance policy in force. But it's a good idea, every five years or so, to increase the amount of insurance in relation to the appreciation of the value of the real estate. As

an example: If a home was purchased five years ago for $40,000 and the present market value is $50,000 the owner should purchase an extra $10,000 in title insurance. Otherwise, if a claim is filed against him the title company will reimburse the owner by only $40,000, not the present value of $50,000. The discrepancy can be much greater if the real estate has been in a family for many years. A palatial home could have been purchased at the turn of the century for $5,000 and if maintained would now be worth in excess of $100,000. If a valid claim was entered against such a property, the title-insurance company would pay the owner $5,000, leaving him short $95,000! The cost of purchasing more title insurance is very nominal and also very worthwhile.

In conclusion, it pays to have an owner's title-insurance policy with any real estate that is purchased, just as the vast majority of property owners have done for years. The cost is small in comparison to the benefit received. Title insurance gives the homeowner complete security against loss as well as complete peace of mind.

18

What is Escrow?

Escrow is the process whereby the deed to your property is held by a disinterested third person (bank, title company, etc.). This third person is also holding the monies paid by the purchaser for your home. This escrow holder, as he is called, will deliver the monies to you, the seller, and then simultaneously deliver the deed to the purchaser at the completion of certain conditions that both you and the purchaser have agreed upon, such as the payment for work done by a contractor (called a mechanic's lien). From the moment that the instrument is actually delivered, the seller's rights stop and the purchaser becomes entitled to all the rights conveyed by the deed.

In some states, escrow companies specialize in such services. Commercial banks, savings and loan associations, and other financial institutions often arrange for delivery in escrow to protect the security of their loan and to accommodate their depositor needs. Frequently, attorneys serve as escrow agents when one or both parties live out of the area or find it too inconvenient to be at the closing in person. Whether the title is

closed in escrow or conventionally with both seller and purchaser in attendance, the various details of the closing, including the proration of income and charge, are basically not affected. When delivery is being made in escrow, all of the money, deeds, and other instruments to be exchanged by the escrow holder are prepared well in advance and held in trust until the closing.

■ Basically, the main advantages of an escrow closing are the following:

(1) The seller will not receive any money until his title is searched and found clear.

(2) When clear title is brought down, the seller is certain that he will be paid and that the escrow contract will be carried out to completion.

(3) It is not necessary for either buyer or seller to be present at the closing of the real estate transaction.

19

The Title Closing

A real estate closing is a meeting at which the seller, buyer, their attorneys, a representative of the title-insurance company, and a representative of the lending institution come together and finalize the transaction in accordance with the contract of sale. At this meeting, the buyer makes all required payouts; all documents necessary for the transfer of title are signed; and, finally, the seller delivers the deed. At that moment, actual title to the home passes to the buyer.

In the normal contract for the sale of real estate, a clause generally provides for the closing at a designated place on a specific day and hour. The date of the closing, as a rule, is four to six weeks after the contract is signed in order to provide ample time for the seller and purchaser to complete the preliminary requirements as set forth in the contract.

Many details must be attended to prior to the actual closing. The responsibility for the fulfillment of these details will rest mainly on the real estate lawyers, the title company and the bankers involved in the transaction. These functions usually include prorations of interest, taxes, insurance and rents; removing existing encumberances; paying off loans of record; the purchaser's obtaining a new mortgage; ordering an abstract of title and purchasing a title-insurance policy. A postponement of the closing commonly occurs because of a delay in completing the examination of title.

Since the exact amount owed by the purchaser is not known until the day of closing, he brings with him a certified check in an amount approximating the sum to be paid. The balance can be paid in cash or with a personal check.

The buyer and seller and their attorneys review the prorations and adjustments in favor of each of the parties, which have been set forth on a closing statement. Among the adjustments in favor of the seller are such items as taxes, if he paid them in advance; prepaid insurance policies; prepaid water bills; rents from the first of the month to the actual date of the closing, if not collected previously; prepaid interest on a mortgage being assumed and other like items. Among the adjustments in favor of the buyer are rents collected by the seller prior to closing, water bills charged to the tenants in advance, back interest due on an existing mortgage being assumed and other like items.

The closing statement sets forth in detail the actual monies due the seller, the credits due the purchaser and the balance that the purchaser must pay at the closing. Normally, the closing statement is prepared by attorneys for the seller and the buyer.

The method of computing prorations and the date used for the prorations vary with the locality. In many areas the adjustments are made as of the day preceeding the closing. What this means is that the buyer receives the income (if any) and is charged with the expenses incurred beginning with and including the day of the closing. There are also two other probable dates that might be used in the computation of the prorations, depending on the locality: the actual day of closing or the day when the buyer takes possession of the home.

We're not going to go into the actual methods of calculating the taxes, interest, rents and insurance because it's beyond the scope of this book and would tend to put the reader to sleep. Any questions you might have in this vein will be gladly answered by your real estate attorney at or before the time of closing.

■ The following documents and information should be in the hands of your attorney at the time of closing:

(1) Seller's copy of the real estate sales contract.

(2) The latest tax, water, assessment, gas and electric bills. Also, you should be able to prove that they have been paid.

(3) The latest possible meter readings for the water, gas and electric.

(4)   All homeowners insurance policies for fire and liability.

(5)   Assignment of leases (if any).

(6)   Affidavit of title.

(7)   Seller's last deed.

(8)   Deed for the purchaser.

(9)   All documents that the seller has agreed to deliver or prepare.

(10)   Any unrecorded instruments that might affect the title.

(11)   Receipt for the last payment of interest on the mortgage.

(12)   Receipts or statements showing that the following have been paid or satisfied: mechanic's liens, judgments, chattel mortgages (personal-property mortgage) or mortgages that must be paid prior to closing.

(13)   Any agreements that have been called for in the contract.

(14)   A certificate from the lending institution showing the amount due on the mortgage and the date to which interest is paid.

(15)   If it is an income property, the seller must turn over a list of the names of the tenants, the amounts of the rents that have been paid and that are still unpaid, the dates when rents are due and an assignment of all unpaid rents.

(16)   The seller must have prepared letters to each of the tenants stating that they are to pay all future rents to the purchaser.

(17)   A bill of sale for all personal property covered in the real estate sales contract.

It's very probable that some of the above items won't be necessary at your particular closing. Your attorney will notify you of exactly what information and documents he needs. And if there are certain areas or terms in the closing that are somewhat cloudy, he'll be happy to enlighten you.

20

Principle and Interest Tables

Following are principal and interest tables (amortization tables) showing the amount of monthly payments required to retire the principal and pay the interest on loans from $100 to $70,000 at interest rates from 6.5 per cent through 10 per cent in increments of ¼ per cent from 15 years to 40 years.

For example, in order to figure the monthly principal and interest (PI) on $79,800 for 30 years at 9 per cent, just take the payment for $70,000, ($563.24), plus the payment for $9,500 ($76.44), plus the payment for $300 ($2.42). Add them all together and you get a monthly payment of $642.10. Please note that this does not include taxes and insurance, which are normally also part of the monthly payment to the lending institution.

In the back of the mind of every beady-eyed lending institution is the insipid fear that the borrower will inevitably go awry in his financial dealing and not be able to pay either his home insurance or his real estate taxes — and the dire consequences of which, will leave the lender with an unsecured mortgage. Heavens forbid!

In order to prevent a holocaust such as this, many lending institutions require the borrower to include his insurance and real estate taxes in with his monthly payment of principal and interest (PITI).

As an example, the monthly principal and interest payment on a 30-year mortgage of $40,000 at 8.5 per cent is $307.57. Let's assume further that the borrower's property taxes are $1,100 and that his yearly insurance premium is $100. Together these two items equal $1,200. One-twelfth of this amount is $100. Since the lending institution is building an escrow account for the borrower, his total payment would be $307.57 plus $100, or $407.57. At the end of the year, the account will have enough money to pay the taxes and insurance, thereby eliminating the possibility of a default in the payment of either bill. On all VA and FHA loans the lending institution is required to set up an escrow account for the borrower. In other instances however, the escrow accounts are not automatic and will be done only if the borrower requests it.

MONTHLY PAYMENT

Necessary To Amortize A Loan

LOAN AMOUNT	15 Years	20 Years	25 Years	29 Years	30 Years	35 Years	40 Years
$ 100	.88	.75	.68	.64	.64	.61	.59
200	1.75	1.50	1.36	1.28	1.27	1.21	1.18
300	2.62	2.24	2.03	1.92	1.90	1.82	1.76
400	3.49	2.99	2.71	2.56	2.53	2.42	2.35
500	4.36	3.73	3.38	3.20	3.17	3.03	2.93
1000	8.72	7.46	6.76	6.40	6.33	6.05	5.86
1500	13.07	11.19	10.13	9.59	9.49	9.07	8.79
2000	17.43	14.92	13.51	12.79	12.65	12.09	11.71
2500	21.78	18.64	16.89	15.99	15.81	15.11	14.64
3000	26.14	22.37	20.26	19.18	18.97	18.13	17.57
3500	30.49	26.10	23.64	22.38	22.13	21.15	20.50
4000	34.85	29.83	27.01	25.57	25.29	24.17	23.42
4500	39.20	33.56	30.39	28.77	28.45	27.19	26.35
5000	43.56	37.28	33.77	31.97	31.61	30.21	29.28
5500	47.92	41.04	37.14	35.16	34.77	33.23	32.21
6000	52.27	44.74	40.52	38.36	37.93	36.25	35.13
6500	56.63	48.47	43.89	41.55	41.09	39.28	38.06
7000	60.98	52.20	47.27	44.75	44.25	42.30	40.99
7500	65.34	55.92	50.65	47.95	47.41	45.32	43.91
8000	69.69	59.65	54.02	51.14	50.57	48.34	46.84
8500	74.05	63.38	57.40	54.34	53.73	51.36	49.77
9000	78.40	67.11	60.77	57.53	56.89	54.38	52.70
10000	87.12	74.56	67.53	63.93	63.21	60.42	58.55
20000	174.23	149.12	135.05	127.85	126.42	120.84	117.10
30000	261.34	223.68	202.57	191.77	189.63	181.25	175.64
40000	348.45	298.23	270.09	255.69	252.83	241.67	234.19
50000	435.56	372.79	337.61	319.61	316.04	302.08	292.73
60000	522.67	447.35	405.13	383.53	379.25	362.50	351.28
70000	609.78	521.91	472.65	447.45	442.45	422.91	409.82

MONTHLY PAYMENT

Necessary To Amortize A Loan

LOAN AMOUNT	15 Years	20 Years	25 Years	29 Years	30 Years	35 Years	40 Years
$ 100	.89	.77	.70	.66	.65	.63	.61
200	1.77	1.53	1.39	1.32	1.30	1.25	1.21
300	2.66	2.29	2.08	1.97	1.95	1.87	1.82
400	3.54	3.05	2.77	2.63	2.60	2.49	2.42
500	4.43	3.81	3.46	3.28	3.25	3.11	3.02
1000	8.85	7.61	6.91	6.56	6.49	6.22	6.04
1500	13.28	11.41	10.37	9.84	9.73	9.33	9.06
2000	17.70	15.21	13.82	13.12	12.98	12.43	12.07
2500	22.13	19.01	17.28	16.39	16.22	15.54	15.09
3000	26.55	22.82	20.73	19.67	19.46	18.65	18.11
3500	30.98	26.62	24.19	22.95	22.71	21.75	21.12
4000	35.40	30.42	27.64	26.23	25.95	24.86	24.14
4500	39.83	34.22	31.10	29.51	29.19	27.97	27.16
5000	44.25	38.02	34.55	32.78	32.43	31.08	30.17
5500	48.68	41.83	38.01	36.06	35.68	34.18	33.19
6000	53.10	45.63	41.46	39.34	38.92	37.29	36.21
6500	57.52	49.43	44.91	42.62	42.16	40.40	39.22
7000	61.95	53.23	48.37	45.90	45.41	43.50	42.24
7500	66.37	57.03	51.82	49.17	48.65	46.61	45.26
8000	70.80	60.83	55.28	52.45	51.89	49.72	48.27
8500	75.22	64.64	58.73	55.73	55.14	52.83	51.29
9000	79.65	68.44	62.19	59.01	58.38	55.93	54.31
9500	84.07	72.24	65.64	62.29	61.62	59.04	57.32
10000	88.50	76.04	69.10	65.56	64.86	62.15	60.34
20000	176.99	152.08	138.19	131.12	129.72	124.29	120.68
30000	265.48	228.11	207.28	196.68	194.58	186.43	181.01
40000	353.97	304.15	276.37	262.24	259.44	248.57	241.35
50000	442.46	380.19	345.46	327.80	324.30	310.71	301.68
60000	530.95	456.22	414.55	393.36	389.16	372.85	362.02
70000	619.44	532.26	483.64	458.91	454.02	435.00	422.35

MONTHLY PAYMENT

Necessary To Amortize A Loan

LOAN AMOUNT	15 Years	20 Years	25 Years	29 Years	30 Years	35 Years	40 Years
$ 100	.90	.78	.71	.68	.67	.64	.63
200	1.80	1.56	1.42	1.35	1.34	1.28	1.25
300	2.70	2.33	2.13	2.02	2.00	1.92	1.87
400	3.60	3.11	2.83	2.69	2.67	2.56	2.49
500	4.50	3.88	3.54	3.37	3.33	3.20	3.11
1000	8.99	7.76	7.07	6.73	6.66	6.39	6.22
1500	13.49	11.63	10.61	10.09	9.98	9.59	9.33
2000	17.98	15.51	14.14	13.45	13.31	12.78	12.43
2500	22.48	19.39	17.67	16.81	16.64	15.98	15.54
3000	26.97	23.26	21.21	20.17	19.96	19.17	18.65
3500	31.46	27.14	24.74	23.53	23.29	22.36	21.76
4000	35.96	31.02	28.28	26.89	26.62	25.56	24.86
4500	40.45	34.89	31.81	30.25	29.94	28.75	27.97
5000	44.95	38.77	35.34	33.61	33.27	31.95	31.08
5500	49.44	42.65	38.88	36.97	36.60	35.14	34.18
6000	53.93	46.52	42.41	40.33	39.92	38.34	37.29
6500	58.43	50.40	45.95	43.69	43.25	41.53	40.40
7000	62.92	54.28	49.48	47.05	46.58	44.72	43.51
7500	67.42	58.15	53.01	50.41	49.90	47.92	46.61
8000	71.91	62.03	56.55	53.78	53.23	51.11	49.72
8500	76.41	65.91	60.08	57.14	56.56	54.31	52.83
9000	80.90	69.78	63.62	60.50	59.88	57.50	55.93
9500	85.39	73.66	67.15	63.86	63.21	60.70	59.04
10000	89.89	77.53	70.68	67.22	66.54	63.89	62.15
20000	179.77	155.06	141.36	134.43	133.07	127.78	124.29
30000	269.65	232.59	212.04	201.64	199.60	191.66	186.43
40000	359.54	310.12	282.72	268.86	266.13	255.55	248.58
50000	449.42	387.65	353.39	336.07	332.66	319.43	310.72
60000	539.30	465.18	424.07	403.28	399.19	383.32	372.86
70000	629.18	542.71	494.75	470.50	465.72	447.20	435.01

MONTHLY PAYMENT

Necessary To Amortize A Loan

LOAN AMOUNT	15 Years	20 Years	25 Years	29 Years	30 Years	35 Years	40 Years
$ 100	.92	.80	.73	.69	.69	.66	.64
200	1.83	1.59	1.45	1.38	1.37	1.32	1.28
300	2.74	2.38	2.17	2.07	2.05	1.97	1.92
400	3.66	3.17	2.90	2.76	2.73	2.63	2.56
500	4.57	3.96	3.62	3.45	3.42	3.29	3.20
1000	9.13	7.91	7.23	6.89	6.83	6.57	6.40
1500	13.70	11.86	10.85	10.34	10.24	9.85	9.60
2000	18.26	15.81	14.46	13.78	13.65	13.13	12.80
2500	22.83	19.76	18.08	17.23	17.06	16.42	16.00
3000	27.39	23.72	21.69	20.67	20.47	19.70	19.20
3500	31.96	27.67	25.30	24.11	23.88	22.98	22.39
4000	36.52	31.62	28.92	27.56	27.29	26.26	25.59
4500	41.08	35.57	32.53	31.00	30.70	29.55	28.79
5000	45.65	39.52	36.15	34.45	34.11	32.83	31.99
5500	50.21	43.48	39.76	37.89	37.52	36.11	35.19
6000	54.78	47.43	43.37	41.34	40.94	39.39	38.39
6500	59.34	51.38	46.99	44.78	44.35	42.68	41.58
7000	63.91	55.33	50.60	48.22	47.76	45.96	44.78
7500	68.47	59.28	54.22	51.67	51.17	49.24	47.98
8000	73.03	63.24	57.83	55.11	54.58	52.52	51.18
8500	77.60	67.19	61.44	58.56	57.99	55.80	54.38
9000	82.16	71.14	65.06	62.00	61.40	59.09	57.58
9500	86.73	75.09	68.67	65.45	64.81	62.37	60.77
10000	91.29	79.04	72.29	68.89	68.22	65.65	63.97
20000	182.58	158.08	144.57	137.77	136.44	131.30	127.94
30000	273.86	237.12	216.85	206.66	204.66	196.95	191.91
40000	365.15	316.16	289.13	275.54	272.88	262.59	255.87
50000	456.44	395.19	361.41	344.43	341.09	328.24	319.84
60000	547.72	474.23	433.69	413.31	409.31	393.89	383.81
70000	639.01	553.27	505.97	482.20	477.53	459.53	447.78

MONTHLY PAYMENT

Necessary To Amortize A Loan   7.5%

LOAN AMOUNT	15 Years	20 Years	25 Years	29 Years	30 Years	35 Years	40 Years
$ 100	.93	.81	.74	.71	.70	.68	.66
200	1.86	1.62	1.48	1.42	1.40	1.35	1.32
300	2.79	2.42	2.22	2.12	2.10	2.03	1.98
400	3.71	3.23	2.96	2.83	2.80	2.70	2.64
500	4.64	4.03	3.70	3.53	3.50	3.38	3.30
1000	9.28	8.06	7.39	7.06	7.00	6.75	6.59
1500	13.91	12.09	11.09	10.59	10.49	10.12	9.88
2000	18.55	16.12	14.78	14.12	13.99	13.49	13.17
2500	23.18	20.14	18.48	17.65	17.49	16.86	16.46
3000	27.82	24.17	22.17	21.18	20.98	20.23	19.75
3500	32.45	28.20	25.87	24.71	24.48	23.60	23.04
4000	37.09	32.23	29.56	28.23	27.97	26.97	26.33
4500	41.72	36.26	33.26	31.76	31.47	30.35	29.62
5000	46.36	40.28	36.95	35.29	34.97	33.72	32.91
5500	50.99	44.31	40.65	38.82	38.46	37.09	36.20
6000	55.63	48.34	44.34	42.35	41.96	40.46	39.49
6500	60.26	52.37	48.04	45.88	45.45	43.83	42.78
7000	64.90	56.40	51.73	49.41	48.95	47.20	46.07
7500	69.53	60.42	55.43	52.93	52.45	50.57	49.36
8000	74.17	64.45	59.12	56.46	55.94	53.94	52.65
8500	78.80	68.48	62.82	59.99	59.44	57.32	55.94
9000	83.44	72.51	66.51	63.52	62.93	60.69	59.23
9500	88.07	76.54	70.21	67.05	66.43	64.06	62.52
10000	92.71	80.56	73.90	70.58	69.93	67.43	65.81
20000	185.41	161.12	149.93	141.15	139.85	134.85	131.62
30000	278.11	241.68	221.70	211.72	209.77	202.28	197.43
40000	370.81	322.24	295.60	282.29	279.69	269.70	263.23
50000	463.51	402.80	369.50	352.87	349.61	337.13	329.04
60000	556.21	483.36	443.40	423.44	419.53	404.55	394.85
70000	648.91	563.92	517.30	494.01	489.46	471.97	460.65

MONTHLY PAYMENT

Necessary To Amortize A Loan

LOAN AMOUNT	15 Years	20 Years	25 Years	29 Years	30 Years	35 Years	40 Years
$ 100	.95	.83	.76	.73	.72	.70	.68
200	1.89	1.65	1.52	1.45	1.44	1.39	1.36
300	2.83	2.47	2.27	2.17	2.15	2.08	2.03
400	3.77	3.29	3.03	2.90	2.87	2.77	2.71
500	4.71	4.11	3.78	3.62	3.59	3.47	3.39
1000	9.42	8.21	7.56	7.23	7.17	6.93	6.77
1500	14.12	12.32	11.33	10.85	10.75	10.39	10.15
2000	18.83	16.42	15.11	14.46	14.33	13.85	13.54
2500	23.54	20.53	18.89	18.07	17.92	17.31	16.92
3000	28.24	24.63	22.66	21.69	21.50	20.77	20.30
3500	32.95	28.74	26.44	25.30	25.08	24.23	23.69
4000	37.66	32.84	30.22	28.92	28.66	27.69	27.07
4500	42.36	36.95	33.99	32.53	32.24	31.15	30.45
5000	47.07	41.05	37.77	36.14	35.83	34.61	33.84
5500	51.78	45.16	41.55	39.76	39.41	38.07	37.22
6000	56.48	49.26	45.32	43.37	42.99	41.54	40.60
6500	61.19	53.37	49.10	46.98	46.57	45.00	43.99
7000	65.89	57.47	52.88	50.60	50.15	48.46	47.37
7500	70.60	61.58	56.65	54.21	53.74	51.92	50.75
8000	75.31	65.68	60.43	57.83	57.32	55.38	54.13
8500	80.01	69.79	64.21	61.44	60.90	58.84	57.52
9000	84.72	73.89	67.98	65.05	64.48	62.30	60.90
9500	89.43	78.00	71.76	68.67	68.06	65.76	64.28
10000	94.13	82.10	75.54	72.28	71.65	69.22	67.67
20000	188.26	164.19	151.07	144.56	143.29	138.44	135.33
30000	282.39	246.29	226.60	216.83	214.93	207.66	202.99
40000	376.52	328.38	302.14	289.11	286.57	276.88	270.65
50000	470.64	410.48	377.67	361.38	358.21	346.09	338.31
60000	564.77	492.57	453.20	433.66	429.85	415.31	405.98
70000	658.90	574.67	528.74	505.93	501.49	484.53	473.64

MONTHLY PAYMENT

Necessary To Amortize A Loan

LOAN AMOUNT	15 Years	20 Years	25 Years	29 Years	30 Years	35 Years	40 Years
$ 100	.96	.84	.78	.74	.74	.72	.70
200	1.92	1.68	1.55	1.48	1.47	1.43	1.40
300	2.87	2.51	2.32	2.22	2.21	2.14	2.09
400	3.83	3.35	3.09	2.96	2.94	2.85	2.79
500	4.78	4.19	3.86	3.70	3.67	3.56	3.48
1000	9.56	8.37	7.72	7.40	7.34	7.11	6.96
1500	14.34	12.55	11.58	11.10	11.01	10.66	10.43
2000	19.12	16.73	15.44	14.80	14.68	14.21	13.91
2500	23.90	20.92	19.30	18.50	18.35	17.76	17.39
3000	28.67	25.10	23.16	22.20	22.02	21.31	20.86
3500	33.45	29.28	27.02	25.90	25.69	24.86	24.34
4000	38.23	33.46	30.88	29.60	29.36	28.42	27.82
4500	43.01	37.64	34.74	33.30	33.02	31.97	31.29
5000	47.79	41.83	38.60	37.00	36.69	35.52	34.77
5500	52.57	46.01	42.45	40.70	40.36	39.07	38.25
6000	57.34	50.19	46.31	44.40	44.03	42.62	41.72
6500	62.12	54.37	50.17	48.10	47.70	46.17	45.20
7000	66.90	58.56	54.03	51.80	51.37	49.72	48.68
7500	71.68	62.74	57.89	55.50	55.04	53.27	52.15
8000	76.46	66.92	61.75	59.20	58.71	56.83	55.63
8500	81.24	71.10	65.61	62.90	62.37	60.38	59.11
9000	86.01	75.28	69.47	66.60	66.04	63.93	62.58
9500	90.79	79.47	73.33	70.30	69.71	67.48	66.06
10000	95.57	83.65	77.19	74.00	73.38	71.03	69.54
20000	191.14	167.29	154.37	147.99	146.76	142.06	139.07
30000	286.70	250.94	231.55	221.99	220.13	213.08	208.60
40000	382.27	334.58	308.73	295.98	293.51	284.11	278.13
50000	477.83	418.23	385.91	369.98	366.89	355.14	347.66
60000	573.40	501.87	463.09	443.97	440.26	426.16	417.19
70000	668.96	585.51	540.28	517.97	513.64	497.19	486.72

MONTHLY PAYMENT

Necessary To Amortize A Loan

LOAN AMOUNT	15 Years	20 Years	25 Years	29 Years	30 Years	35 Years	40 Years
$ 100	.98	.86	.79	.76	.76	.73	.72
200	1.95	1.71	1.58	1.52	1.51	1.46	1.43
300	2.92	2.56	2.37	2.28	2.26	2.19	2.15
400	3.89	3.41	3.16	3.03	3.01	2.92	2.86
500	4.86	4.27	3.95	3.79	3.76	3.65	3.58
1000	9.71	8.53	7.89	7.58	7.52	7.29	7.15
1500	14.56	12.79	11.83	11.36	11.27	10.93	10.72
2000	19.41	17.05	15.77	15.15	15.03	14.57	14.29
2500	24.26	21.31	19.72	18.94	18.79	18.22	17.86
3000	29.11	25.57	23.66	22.72	22.54	21.86	21.43
3500	33.96	29.83	27.60	26.51	26.30	25.50	25.00
4000	38.81	34.09	31.54	30.30	30.06	29.14	28.57
4500	43.66	38.35	35.49	34.08	33.81	32.79	32.14
5000	48.51	42.61	39.43	37.87	37.57	36.43	35.71
5500	53.36	46.87	43.37	41.66	41.32	40.07	39.28
6000	58.21	51.13	47.31	45.44	45.08	43.71	42.85
6500	63.06	55.39	51.25	49.23	48.84	47.36	46.42
7000	67.91	59.65	55.20	53.01	52.59	51.00	49.99
7500	72.77	63.91	59.14	56.80	56.35	54.64	53.57
8000	77.62	68.17	63.08	60.59	60.11	58.28	57.14
8500	82.47	72.43	67.02	64.37	63.86	61.93	60.71
9000	87.32	76.69	70.97	68.16	67.62	65.57	64.28
9500	92.17	80.95	74.91	71.95	71.38	69.21	67.85
10000	97.02	85.21	78.85	75.73	75.13	72.85	71.42
20000	194.03	170.42	157.70	151.46	150.26	145.70	142.83
30000	291.05	255.62	236.54	227.19	225.38	218.55	214.25
40000	388.06	340.83	315.39	302.92	300.51	291.40	285.66
50000	485.08	426.04	394.23	378.65	375.64	364.25	357.07
60000	582.09	511.24	473.08	454.38	450.76	437.10	428.49
70000	679.10	596.45	551.92	530.10	525.89	509.95	499.90

MONTHLY PAYMENT

        Necessary To Amortize A Loan

LOAN AMOUNT	15 Years	20 Years	25 Years	29 Years	30 Years	35 Years	40 Years
$ 100	.99	.87	.81	.78	.77	.75	.74
200	1.97	1.74	1.62	1.55	1.54	1.50	1.47
300	2.96	2.61	2.42	2.33	2.31	2.25	2.20
400	3.94	3.48	3.23	3.10	3.08	2.99	2.94
500	4.93	4.34	4.03	3.88	3.85	3.74	3.67
1000	9.85	8.68	8.06	7.75	7.69	7.47	7.34
1500	14.78	13.02	12.08	11.63	11.54	11.21	11.00
2000	19.70	17.36	16.11	15.50	15.38	14.94	14.67
2500	24.62	21.70	20.14	19.37	19.23	18.68	18.33
3000	29.55	26.04	24.16	23.25	23.07	22.41	22.00
3500	34.47	30.38	28.19	27.12	26.92	26.15	25.66
4000	39.39	34.72	32.21	31.00	30.76	29.88	29.33
4500	44.32	39.06	36.24	34.87	34.61	33.61	32.99
5000	49.24	43.40	40.27	38.74	38.45	37.35	36.66
5500	54.17	47.74	44.29	42.62	42.30	41.08	40.33
6000	59.09	52.07	48.32	46.49	46.14	44.82	43.99
6500	64.01	56.41	52.34	50.37	49.98	48.55	47.66
7000	68.94	60.75	56.37	54.24	53.83	52.29	51.32
7500	73.86	65.09	60.40	58.11	57.67	56.02	54.99
8000	78.78	69.43	64.42	61.99	61.52	59.75	58.65
8500	83.71	73.77	68.45	65.86	65.36	63.49	62.32
9000	88.63	78.11	72.48	69.73	69.21	67.22	65.98
9500	93.56	82.45	76.50	73.61	73.05	70.96	69.65
10000	98.48	86.79	80.53	77.48	76.90	74.69	73.31
20000	196.95	173.57	161.05	154.96	153.79	149.38	146.62
30000	295.43	260.35	241.57	232.44	230.68	224.06	219.93
40000	393.90	347.13	322.10	309.91	307.57	298.75	293.24
50000	492.37	433.92	402.62	387.39	384.46	373.44	366.55
60000	590.85	520.70	483.14	464.87	461.35	448.12	439.86
70000	689.32	607.48	563.66	542.34	538.24	522.81	513.17

MONTHLY PAYMENT

Necessary To Amortize A Loan

LOAN AMOUNT	15 Years	20 Years	25 Years	29 Years	30 Years	35 Years	40 Years
$ 100	1.00	.89	.83	.80	.79	.77	.76
200	2.00	1.77	1.65	1.59	1.58	1.54	1.51
300	3.00	2.66	2.47	2.38	2.37	2.30	2.26
400	4.00	3.54	3.29	3.17	3.15	3.07	3.01
500	5.00	4.42	4.12	3.97	3.94	3.83	3.77
1000	10.00	8.84	8.23	7.93	7.87	7.66	7.53
1500	15.00	13.26	12.34	11.89	11.81	11.49	11.29
2000	19.99	17.68	16.45	15.85	15.74	15.31	15.05
2500	24.99	22.10	20.56	19.81	19.67	19.14	18.81
3000	29.99	26.52	24.67	23.78	23.61	22.97	22.57
3500	34.99	30.93	28.78	27.74	27.54	26.79	26.33
4000	39.98	35.35	32.89	31.70	31.47	30.62	30.09
4500	44.98	39.77	37.00	35.66	35.41	34.45	33.85
5000	49.98	44.19	41.11	39.62	39.34	38.27	37.61
5500	54.97	48.61	45.22	43.59	43.27	42.10	41.37
6000	59.97	53.03	49.33	47.55	47.21	45.93	45.14
6500	64.97	57.45	53.44	51.51	51.14	49.75	48.90
7000	69.97	61.86	57.56	55.47	55.07	53.58	52.66
7500	74.96	66.28	61.67	59.43	59.01	57.41	56.42
8000	79.96	70.70	65.78	63.40	62.94	61.23	60.18
8500	84.96	75.12	69.89	67.36	66.87	65.06	63.94
9000	89.96	79.54	74.00	71.32	70.81	68.89	67.70
9500	94.95	83.96	78.11	75.28	74.74	72.71	71.46
10000	99.95	88.38	82.22	79.24	78.68	76.54	75.22
20000	199.89	176.75	164.43	158.48	157.35	153.08	150.44
30000	299.84	265.12	246.65	237.72	236.02	229.61	225.66
40000	399.78	353.49	328.86	316.96	314.69	306.15	300.87
50000	499.73	441.86	411.08	396.20	393.36	382.69	376.09
60000	599.67	530.23	493.29	475.44	472.03	459.22	451.31
70000	699.62	618.60	575.51	554.68	550.70	535.76	526.52

MONTHLY PAYMENT

Necessary To Amortize A Loan

LOAN AMOUNT	15 Years	20 Years	25 Years	29 Years	30 Years	35 Years	40 Years
$ 100	1.02	.90	.84	.82	.81	.79	.78
200	2.03	1.80	1.68	1.63	1.61	1.57	1.55
300	3.05	2.70	2.52	2.44	2.42	2.36	2.32
400	4.06	3.60	3.36	3.25	3.22	3.14	3.09
500	5.08	4.50	4.20	4.06	4.03	3.92	3.86
1000	10.15	9.00	8.40	8.11	8.05	7.84	7.72
1500	15.22	13.50	12.59	12.16	12.07	11.76	11.58
2000	20.29	18.00	16.79	16.21	16.10	15.68	15.43
2500	25.36	22.50	20.98	20.26	20.12	19.60	19.29
3000	30.43	27.00	25.18	24.31	24.14	23.52	23.15
3500	35.50	31.50	29.38	28.36	28.17	27.44	27.00
4000	40.58	35.99	33.57	32.41	32.19	31.36	30.86
4500	45.65	40.49	37.77	36.46	36.21	35.28	34.72
5000	50.72	44.99	41.96	40.51	40.24	39.20	38.57
5500	55.79	49.49	46.16	44.56	44.26	43.12	42.43
6000	60.86	53.99	50.36	48.61	48.28	47.04	46.29
6500	65.93	58.49	54.55	52.67	52.31	50.96	50.14
7000	71.00	62.99	58.75	56.72	56.33	54.88	54.00
7500	76.07	67.48	62.49	60.77	60.35	58.80	57.86
8000	81.15	71.98	67.14	64.82	64.37	62.72	61.71
8500	86.22	76.48	71.34	68.87	68.40	66.64	65.57
9000	91.29	80.98	75.53	72.92	72.42	70.56	69.43
9500	96.36	85.48	79.73	76.97	76.44	74.48	73.28
10000	101.43	89.98	83.92	81.02	80.47	78.40	77.14
20000	202.86	179.95	167.84	162.04	160.93	156.80	154.28
30000	304.28	269.92	251.76	243.05	241.39	235.20	231.41
40000	405.71	359.90	335.68	324.07	321.85	313.60	308.55
50000	507.14	449.87	419.60	405.08	402.32	392.00	385.69
60000	608.56	539.84	503.52	486.10	482.78	470.40	462.82
70000	709.99	629.81	587.44	567.12	563.24	548.80	539.96

MONTHLY PAYMENT

Necessary To Amortize A Loan 9.25%

LOAN AMOUNT	15 Years	20 Years	25 Years	29 Years	30 Years	35 Years	40 Years
$ 100	1.03	.92	.86	.83	.83	.81	.80
200	2.06	1.84	1.72	1.66	1.65	1.61	1.59
300	3.09	2.75	2.57	2.49	2.47	2.41	2.38
400	4.12	3.67	3.43	3.32	3.30	3.22	3.17
500	5.15	4.58	4.29	4.15	4.12	4.02	3.96
1000	10.30	9.16	8.57	8.29	8.23	8.03	7.91
1500	15.44	13.74	12.85	12.43	12.35	12.05	11.86
2000	20.59	18.32	17.13	16.57	16.46	16.06	15.82
2500	25.73	22.90	21.41	20.71	20.57	20.07	19.77
3000	30.88	27.48	25.70	24.85	24.69	24.09	23.72
3500	36.03	32.06	29.98	28.99	28.80	28.10	27.68
4000	41.17	36.64	34.26	33.13	32.91	32.11	31.63
4500	46.32	41.22	38.54	37.27	37.03	36.13	35.58
5000	51.46	45.80	42.82	41.41	41.14	40.14	39.54
5500	56.61	50.38	47.11	45.55	45.25	44.16	43.49
6000	61.76	54.96	51.39	49.69	49.37	48.17	47.44
6500	66.90	59.54	55.67	53.83	53.48	52.18	51.40
7000	71.05	64.12	59.95	57.97	57.59	56.20	55.35
7500	77.19	68.70	64.23	62.11	61.71	60.21	59.30
8000	82.34	73.27	68.52	66.25	65.82	64.22	63.26
8500	87.49	77.85	72.80	70.39	69.93	68.24	67.21
9000	92.63	82.43	77.08	74.53	74.05	72.25	71.16
9500	97.78	87.01	81.36	78.67	78.16	76.27	75.12
10000	102.92	91.59	85.64	82.81	82.27	80.28	79.07
20000	205.84	183.18	171.28	165.62	164.54	160.55	158.14
30000	308.76	274.77	256.92	248.42	246.81	240.83	237.20
40000	411.68	366.35	342.56	331.23	329.08	321.10	316.27
50000	514.60	457.94	428.20	414.03	411.34	401.38	395.34
60000	617.52	549.53	513.83	496.84	493.61	481.65	474.40
70000	720.44	641.11	599.47	579.64	575.88	561.93	553.47

MONTHLY PAYMENT

Necessary To Amortize A Loan

LOAN AMOUNT	15 Years	20 Years	25 Years	29 Years	30 Years	35 Years	40 Years
$ 100	1.05	.94	.88	.85	.85	.83	.82
200	2.09	1.87	1.75	1.70	1.69	1.65	1.63
300	3.14	2.80	2.63	2.54	2.53	2.47	2.44
400	4.18	3.73	3.50	3.39	3.37	3.29	3.25
500	5.23	4.67	4.37	4.24	4.21	4.11	4.06
1000	10.45	9.33	8.74	8.47	8.41	8.22	8.11
1500	15.67	13.99	13.11	12.70	12.62	12.33	12.16
2000	20.89	18.65	17.48	16.93	16.82	16.44	16.21
2500	26.11	23.31	21.85	21.16	21.03	20.55	20.26
3000	31.33	27.97	26.22	25.39	25.23	24.65	24.31
3500	36.55	32.63	30.58	29.62	29.43	28.76	28.36
4000	41.77	37.29	34.95	33.85	33.64	32.87	32.41
4500	47.00	41.95	39.32	38.08	37.84	36.98	36.46
5000	52.22	46.61	43.69	42.31	42.05	41.09	40.51
5500	57.44	51.27	48.06	46.54	46.25	45.19	44.56
6000	62.66	55.93	52.43	50.77	50.46	49.30	48.61
6500	67.88	60.59	56.80	55.00	54.66	53.41	52.66
7000	73.10	65.25	61.16	59.23	58.86	57.52	56.71
7500	78.32	69.91	65.53	63.46	63.07	61.63	60.76
8000	83.54	74.58	69.90	67.69	67.27	65.73	64.81
8500	88.76	79.24	74.27	71.92	71.48	69.84	68.86
9000	93.99	83.90	78.64	76.15	75.68	73.95	72.91
9500	99.21	88.56	83.01	80.38	79.89	78.06	76.96
10000	104.43	93.22	87.37	84.61	84.09	82.17	81.01
20000	208.85	186.43	174.74	169.22	168.18	164.33	162.02
30000	313.27	279.64	262.11	253.83	252.26	246.49	243.02
40000	417.69	372.86	349.48	338.43	336.35	328.65	324.03
50000	522.12	466.07	436.85	423.04	420.43	410.81	405.04
60000	626.54	559.28	524.22	507.65	504.52	492.97	486.04
70000	730.96	652.50	611.59	592.26	588.60	575.13	567.05

MONTHLY PAYMENT

Necessary To Amortize A Loan

LOAN AMOUNT	15 Years	20 Years	25 Years	29 Years	30 Years	35 Years	40 Years
$ 100	1.06	.95	.90	.87	.86	.85	.83
200	2.12	1.90	1.79	1.73	1.72	1.69	1.66
300	3.18	2.85	2.68	2.60	2.58	2.53	2.49
400	4.24	3.80	3.57	3.46	3.44	3.37	3.32
500	5.30	4.75	4.46	4.33	4.30	4.21	4.15
1000	10.60	9.49	8.92	8.65	8.60	8.41	8.30
1500	15.90	14.23	13.37	12.97	12.89	12.61	12.45
2000	21.19	18.98	17.83	17.29	17.19	16.82	16.60
2500	26.49	23.72	22.28	21.61	21.48	21.02	20.74
3000	31.79	28.46	26.74	25.93	25.78	25.22	24.89
3500	37.08	33.20	31.19	30.25	30.08	29.43	29.04
4000	42.38	37.95	35.65	34.57	34.37	33.63	33.19
4500	47.68	42.69	40.11	38.89	38.67	37.83	37.34
5000	52.97	47.43	44.56	43.22	42.96	42.03	41.48
5500	58.27	52.17	49.02	47.54	47.26	46.24	45.63
6000	63.57	56.92	53.47	51.86	51.55	50.44	49.78
6500	68.86	61.66	57.93	56.18	55.85	54.64	53.93
7000	74.16	66.40	62.38	60.50	60.15	58.85	58.07
7500	79.46	71.14	66.84	64.82	64.44	63.05	62.22
8000	84.75	75.89	71.30	69.14	68.74	67.25	66.37
8500	90.05	80.63	75.75	73.46	73.03	71.46	70.52
9000	95.35	85.37	80.21	77.78	77.33	75.66	74.67
9500	100.64	90.11	84.66	82.11	81.62	79.86	78.81
10000	105.94	94.86	89.12	86.43	85.92	84.06	82.96
20000	211.88	189.71	178.23	172.85	171.84	168.12	165.92
30000	317.81	284.56	267.35	259.27	257.75	252.18	248.87
40000	423.75	379.41	356.46	345.69	343.67	336.24	331.83
50000	529.69	474.26	445.57	432.11	429.58	420.30	414.78
60000	635.62	569.12	534.69	518.53	515.50	504.36	497.74
70000	741.56	663.97	623.80	604.96	601.41	588.42	580.70

MONTHLY PAYMENT

Necessary To Amortize A Loan

LOAN AMOUNT	15 Years	20 Years	25 Years	29 Years	30 Years	35 Years	40 Years
$ 100	1.08	.97	.91	.89	.88	.86	.85
200	2.15	1.94	1.81	1.77	1.76	1.72	1.70
300	3.23	2.90	2.73	2.65	2.64	2.58	2.55
400	4.30	3.87	3.64	3.53	3.52	3.44	3.40
500	5.38	4.83	4.55	4.42	4.39	4.30	4.25
1000	10.75	9.66	9.09	8.83	8.78	8.60	8.50
1500	16.12	14.48	13.64	13.24	13.17	12.90	12.74
2000	21.50	19.31	18.18	17.65	17.56	17.20	16.99
2500	26.87	24.13	22.72	22.07	21.94	21.50	21.23
3000	32.24	28.96	27.27	26.48	26.33	25.80	25.48
3500	37.62	33.78	31.81	30.89	30.72	30.09	29.73
4000	42.99	38.61	36.35	35.30	35.11	34.39	33.97
4500	48.36	43.43	40.90	39.72	39.50	38.69	38.22
5000	53.74	48.26	45.44	44.13	43.88	42.99	42.46
5500	59.11	53.08	49.98	48.54	48.27	47.29	46.71
6000	64.48	57.91	54.53	52.95	52.66	51.59	50.95
6500	69.85	62.73	59.07	57.37	57.05	55.88	55.20
7000	75.23	67.56	63.61	61.78	61.44	60.18	59.45
7500	80.60	72.38	68.16	66.19	65.82	64.48	63.69
8000	85.97	77.21	72.70	70.60	70.21	68.78	67.94
8500	91.35	82.03	77.24	75.02	74.60	73.08	72.18
9000	96.72	86.86	81.79	79.43	78.99	77.38	76.43
9500	102.09	91.68	86.33	83.84	83.37	81.67	80.67
10000	107.47	96.51	90.88	88.25	87.76	85.97	84.92
20000	214.93	193.01	181.75	176.50	175.52	171.94	169.83
30000	322.39	289.51	272.62	264.75	263.28	257.91	254.75
40000	429.85	386.01	363.49	353.00	351.03	343.87	339.66
50000	537.31	482.52	454.36	441.24	438.79	429.84	424.58
60000	644.77	579.02	545.23	529.49	526.55	515.81	509.49
70000	752.23	675.52	636.10	617.74	614.31	601.78	594.41

21

Glossary

In the following glossary I have tried to include any and all words that pertain to the general sale of real estate. Your lawyer will undoubtedly include many in his conversation with you. The purpose of these words is twofold: (1) to befuddle the listener and (2) to make him feel as though he needs the speaker.

ABSTRACT OF TITLE — A condensed history of the title, consisting of a summary of the different links in the chain of title, together with a statement of all liens, charges, or encumbrances affecting a particular property.

ACRE — A measure of land, 160 square rods, 4,840 square yards, 43,560 square feet.

AD VALOREM — Designates an assessment of taxes against property. Literally, according to the value.

ADVERSE POSSESSION — The right of an occupant of land to acquire title against the real owner, where possession has been actual, continuous, hostile, visible and distinct for the statutory period.

AGENT — One who represents another from whom he has derived authority.

AGREEMENT OF SALE — A written agreement whereby the purchaser agrees to buy certain real estate and the seller agrees to sell upon terms and conditions set forth therein.

AMENITIES — The qualities and state of being pleasant and agreeable. In appraising, those qualities that attach to property in the benefits derived from ownership other than monetary. Satisfactions of possession and use arising from architectural excellence, scenic beauty and social enviroment.

AMORTIZATION — The liquidation of a financial obligation on an installment basis, usually with equal payments at regular intervals over a specific period of time.

APPRAISAL — An estimate of quantity, quality or value. The process through which conclusions of property value are obtained; also refers to the report setting forth the *estimate* of value.

APPRECIATION — An increase in the value of property due to economic causes that may prove to be either temporary or permanent.

APPRECIATION RATE — The "index figure" used against the actual or estimated cost of a property in computing its cost of reproduction as of different date or under different conditions of a higher price level.

APPURTENANCE — That which has been added to another thing; that which has been added or appended to a property and which becomes an inherent part of the property and passes with it when it is sold, leased or devised.

ASSESSED VALUATION — Assessment of real estate by the county assessor for taxation purposes.

ASSESSMENT — A charge against real estate made by a unit of government to cover the proportionate cost of an improvement, such as a street or sewer.

ASSESSOR — One whose duty it is to assess property for taxation.

ASSUMPTION OF MORTGAGE — When a buyer takes ownership to real estate encumbered with a mortgage, he may assume the responsibility as the guarantor for the unpaid balance of the mortgage. Such a buyer is liable for the mortgage repayment.

BINDER — An agreement to cover a down payment for the purchase of real estate as evidence of good faith on the part of the purchaser. In insurance: a temporary agreement given to one having an insurable interest and subject to the same conditions that will apply if, and when a policy is issued.

BLANKET MORTGAGE — A mortgage that has two or more properties pledged as security for a debt, usually for subdividing purposes. A single mortgage that covers more than one piece of real estate.

BREEZEWAY — A covered porch or passage,

open on two sides, connecting house and garage or two parts of the house.

BROKER — One employed by another, for a fee, to carry on any of the activities listed in the license law definition of the word. One who acts as an agent or the representative of others in buying or selling real estate.

BUILDING CODE — Regulating the construction of building within a municipality by ordinance or law.

BUILDING RESTRICTIONS — Limitations on the use of property or the size and location of houses, established by legislation or by covenants in deeds.

BUILT-IN — Any wardrobe, kitchen cabinet or similar feature built as part of the house.

BUNDLE OF RIGHTS — Ownership of a parcel of real estate embraces a great many rights, such as the right to occupancy and use, the right to sell in whole or in part, the right to bequeath, the right to transfer the benefits to be derived by occupancy and use of the real estate. These rights of occupancy and use are called beneficial interests. An owner who leases real estate to a tenant transfers one of the rights in his bundle, namely, the beneficial interests or the right to use or occupancy, to the tenant.

He retains all the other rights in the bundle. As compensation for the temporary relinquishment of the beneficial interest in the real estate, the owner receives rent.

CARPORT — A roof over a section of the driveway, usually extending out from the house.

CERTIFICATE OF TITLE — A document usually given to the home buyer with the deed, stating that title to the property is clear; it is prepared by a title company or an attorney and is based on the abstract of title.

CHATTEL — Personal property, such as household goods or fixtures.

CLOSING STATEMENT — A listing of the debits and credits of the buyer and seller to a real estate transaction for the financial settlement of the transaction.

CLOUD ON THE TITLE — An outstanding claim or encumbrance that if valid, would affect or impair the owner's title; a mortgage or judgment.

COINSURANCE — The coinsurance or average clause in a fire-insurance policy is a device to penalize the underinsured. The most common clauses provide for insurance in the amount of 80 per cent of the value of the building.

COMMISSION — Payment due a real estate broker for services in that capacity. A payment measured by a percentage of another sum — as a percentage of the sale price paid for selling a property.

COMMON PROPERTY — Land generally considered as the property of the public in which all persons enjoy equal rights: a legal term signifying an incorporeal hereditament consisting of a right of one person in the land of another; property not owned by individuals or government but groups or in formal villages.

COMPOUND INTEREST — Interest paid both on the original principal and on interest accrued from the time it fell due.

CONDEMNATION — Taking private property for public use, with compensation to the owner, under the right of eminent domain.

CONDOMINIUM — Full ownership of a part or space unit of developed land and an undivided interest to use the common land or space areas on an equal basis with other condominium owners.

CONSIDERATION — The price that induces a contract: may be in money, or a transfer of personal effort. In appraising, usually the actual price at which property is transferred.

CONSTANT-PAYMENT MORTGAGE — Systematic loan-reduction plan by which the borrower pays a fixed amount each month, part to be applied to repayment of principal and part to payment of interest.

CONSTRUCTION LOAN — A loan to finance the improvement of real estate.

CONTINGENCIES — Possible happenings that are conditioned upon the occurrence of some future event that is itself uncertain or questionable — *i.e.,* an offer to purchase conditioned upon the commitment of a mortgage loan.

CONTINGENT FEES — Remuneration based or conditioned upon future occurrences or conclusions or results of services to be performed.

CONTRACT — An agreement entered into by two or more parties by the terms of which one or more of the parties, for a consideration, undertakes to do or to refrain from doing some act or acts in accordance with the wishes of the other party or parties. A contract to be valid and binding must (1) be entered into by competent parties, (2) be bound by a consideration, (3) possess mutuality, (4) represent an actual meeting of minds, and (5) cover a legal and moral act.

CONTRACT FOR DEED — Very much like a mortgage but may differ from it in important ways. Usually used to evidence the equity of the seller of a piece of property when he fails to receive the entire purchase price either in cash or a purchase-money mortgage.

CONVEYANCE — A written instrument that posses an interest in real estate from one person to another, including land contracts, leases, mortgages, etc.

COOPERATIVE OWNERSHIP — Ownership of shares in a cooperative venture entitling the owner to use, rent or sell a specific space unit (apartment).

CORPOREAL — Pertaining to a right or group of rights of a visible and tangible nature.

COST OF REPRODUCTION — The normal

cost of exact duplication of a property with similar materials.

COVENANT — An agreement between two or more persons, by deed, whereby one of the parties promises the performance or nonperformance of certain acts.

DEDICATION — An appropriation of land by an owner to some public use together with acceptance for such use by or on behalf of the public.

DEED — A writing by which lands, tenements and hereditaments are transferred, when said writing is signed, sealed and delivered by the grantor.

DEFAULT — Failure to meet an obligation when due. Thus, a mortgagor is in default when he fails to pay interest or principal on his mortgage when due.

DEFICIENCY JUDGMENT — The negative difference between the indebtedness and the sale price of the real estate at the foreclosure sale, which the debtor will still owe.

DEPOSIT, OR EARNEST MONEY — A sum of money or other consideration tendered in conjunction with an offer to purchase rights in real property.

DEPRECIATION — Loss in value brought about by deterioration through ordinary wear and tear, action of the elements or functional obsolescence.

DEVISE — A gift of a real property by last will and testament.

DISPOSSESS — To deprive one of the use of real estate.

EARNEST MONEY — Down payment made by a purchaser of real estate as evidence of good faith.

EASEMENT — The right to use or enjoy certain privileges that pertain to the land of another; the right, liberty, advantage or privilege that one individual has in lands of another; a right-of-way.

ECONOMIC LIFE — The period over which a property may be profitably utilized.

EMINENT DOMAIN — The right of the people or government to take private property for public use upon payment of compensation.

ENCROACHMENT — A building, part of building or obstruction that intrudes upon a highway or sidewalk or trespasses upon property of another.

ENCUMBRANCE — A claim, lien, charge or liability attached to and binding upon real property, such as a judgment, unpaid taxes or a right-of-way.

EQUITY — The interest or value that an owner has in real estate over and above the mortgage.

ESCHEAT — Reversion of property to the sovereign state when there aren't any heirs capable of inheriting the property.

ESCROW — A deed delivered to a third person for the grantee to be held by him until the performance of some act or condition.

ESCROW HOLDER — One who receives a deed from a grantor to be delivered to his grantee upon the performance of a condition or the occurrence of a contingency.

ESTATE — A right in property; quantity of interest a person has in property.

EXCLUSIVE AGENCY — The appointment of one real estate broker as sole agent for the sale of a property for a designated period of time.

EXCLUSIVE LISTING — A contract to sell property as an agent, according to the terms of which the agent is given the exclusive right to sell the property of is made the exclusive agent for its sale.

EXISTING MORTGAGE — Mortgage contract in which the seller of a house is mortgagor, which is to be assumed by the purchaser.

FEE SIMPLE — The largest estate or ownership in real property.

FIDUCIARY — The relationship between a person charged with the duty of acting for the benefit of another, as between guardian and ward, or broker and seller.

FIRST MORTGAGE — A mortgage that has priority as a lien over all other mortgages.

FIXTURE — Real fixtures, such as furnaces or plumbing fixtures, that are part of the real estate.

FORCED SALE — The act of selling property under compulsion. Usually a sale made by virtue of a court order, ordinarily at public auction.

FORECLOSURE — A court process instituted by a mortgagee or lien creditor to defeat any interest or redemption that the owner may have in the property.

GI (VA) LOAN — A mortgage loan for which veterans are eligible and which is insured by the Veterans Administration, subject to VA regulations; similar to a FHA loan.

GRANTEE — A person to whom real estate is conveyed; the buyer.

GRANTOR — A person who conveys real estate by deed; the seller.

GUARANTEE SALE — The written commitment by a broker that within a certain period of time he will, in absence of a sale, purchase a given piece of property at a specified sum.

HOMESTEAD — Real estate occupied by the owner as a home; the owner enjoys special rights and privileges.

INSTALLMENT CONTRACT — See LAND CONTRACT.

INTEREST RATE — The percentage of the principal sum charged for its use.

JOINT TENANCY — A property shared by two or more persons with the right of survivorship.

JUDGMENT — Decree of court declaring that one individual is indebted to another and fixing the amount of such indebtedness.

JUNIOR LIEN — A lien placed on property after a previous lien has been made and recorded.

JUNIOR MORTGAGE — A mortgage second in lien to a previous mortgage.

LAND CONTRACT, or INSTALLMENT CONTRACT — A contract given to a purchaser of real estate who pays a small portion of the purchase price when the contract is signed, but agrees to pay additional sums, at intervals and in amounts specified in the contract, until the total purchase price is paid and the seller gives a deed; upon default, payments are forefeited.

LEASE — A contract written or oral, for the possession of lands and tenements, on the one hand, and a recompense of rent or other income, on the other.

LEGAL DESCRIPTION — A statement containing a designation by which land is identified according to a system approved by law.

LIEN — A hold or claim that one person has upon property of another; a security for a debt or charge; judgments, mortgages, taxes.

LIFE ESTATE — An estate or interest held during the term of some certain person's life.

LISTING — A record of property for sale by a broker who has been authorized by the owner to sell; oral or written employment of broker by owner to sell or lease real estate.

MARKET VALUE — The highest price that a buyer, willing but not compelled to buy, would pay, and the lowest a seller, willing but not compelled to sell, would accept.

MECHANIC'S LIEN — A lien in favor of persons who have performed work or furnished materials in the erection or repair of a building.

METES AND BOUNDS — A description in a deed of the land location in which the boundaries are defined by directions and distances.

MORTGAGE — A conditional transfer or conveyance of real property as security for the payment of a debt or the fulfillment of some obligation.

MORTGAGEE — A person to whom property is conveyed as security for a loan (the creditor).

MORTGAGOR — An owner who conveys his property as security for a loan (the debtor).

MULTIPLE LISTING — The arrangement among real estate board members whereby each broker brings his listings to the attention of the other members so that, if a sale results, the commission is divided between the broker bringing the listing and the broker making the sale, with a small percentage going to the multiple listing board.

NET LISTING — A price, which must be expressly agreed upon, below which the owner will not sell the property and at which price the broker will not receive a commission; the broker receives the excess over and above the net listing as his commission. The excess must represent a *reasonable* brokerage charge otherwise it can constitute fraud on the part of the broker.

NONCONFORMING USE — A use that was lawfully established but that, because of the application of a zoning ordinance to it, no longer conforms to the regulations of the area in which it is located. A nonconforming building constitutes a nonconforming use of the land upon which it is located.

NOTE — An instrument of credit given to evidence a debt.

OBSOLESCENCE — Impairment of desirability and usefullness brought about by physical, economic or from external influencing circumstances that make a property less desirable and valuable for a continuity or use.

OPEN-HOUSING LAW — A law passed by Congress in April 1968 prohibiting discrimination in the sale of real estate because of race, color or religion of buyers in certain situations (see text).

OPEN-END MORTGAGE — A mortgage with a clause giving the mortgagor the privilege of borrowing additional money after the loan has been reduced, without rewriting the mortgage.

OPEN LISTING — An oral or general listing.

OPINION OF TITLE — Legal opinion stating that title to the property is clear and marketable; serves the same purpose as a certificate of title.

OPTION — An agreement granting the right to purchase or lease a property during a stated period of time, without creating any obligation, to purchase, sell or otherwise direct or contract the use of a property, for which right, a consideration is paid.

OVERIMPROVEMENT — An improvement that is not the best use for the site on which it is placed by reason of excess in size or cost.

PARTITION — Act of dividing property among the several owners. They may hold the real estate in either joint tenancy or as tenants in common.

PARTY WALL — A dividing wall erected over a line separating two adjoining properties and in which the owners of the respective parcels have common rights to its use.

PERFORMANCE BOND — A bond to guarantee specific completion of an undertaking in accordance with an agreement, such as that supplied by a contractor guaranteeing the completion of a building.

POLICE POWER — The inherent right of a government to pass such legislation as may be necessary to protect the public health and safety and to promote the general welfare.

PRINCIPAL — A sum lent as investment, as distinguished from its income; the original amount of the total due and payable at a certain date.

PRINCIPAL NOTE — The promissory note that is secured by the mortgage or trust deed.

PROPERTY — The right that an individual has in lands and chattels to the exclusion of all others.

PURCHASE-MONEY MORTGAGE — A mortgage that is executed by the purchaser as a part of the purchase price.

QUITCLAIM DEED — A deed given when the grantee already has, or claims, complete or partial title to the premises and the grantor has a possible interest that otherwise would constitute a cloud upon the title.

REAL ESTATE BROKER — Any person, firm, partnership or corporation who for a compensation sells or offers for sale, buys or offers to buy, or negotiates the purchase or sale or exchange of real estate, or who leases or offers to lease or rents or offers for rent any real estate or the improvements thereon for others.

REAL ESTATE SALESMAN — Any person who for a compensation has contracted with a real estate broker to sell or offer to sell or to buy or offer to buy or negotiate the purchase or sale or exchange of real estate, or to lease, to rent, or offer for rent any real estate, or to negotiate leases thereof, or of the improvement thereon.

REAL ESTATE TAX — A charge laid upon real property for public purposes.

REALTOR — A coined (patented) word to designate a real estate broker affiliated with the State and National Association of Real Estate Boards.

REALTY — Used as a synonym for real estate.

RELEASE OF LIEN — The discharge of a property from the lien of a judgment, mortgage or claim.

REMAINDER ESTATE — An estate in property created at the same time by the same instrument as another estate and limited to begin immediately upon the termination of the other estate.

REPRODUCTION COST — Normal cost of exact duplication of a property, as of a certain date.

RESTRICTION — A device in a deed for controlling the use of land for the benefit of the land or other invested interests.

REVENUE STAMPS — Adhesive stamps issued by the federal or a state government, which must be purchased and affixed, in amounts provided by law, to deeds of conveyances.

SALES CONTRACT — A contract embodying the terms of agreement of a sale.

SATISFACTION PIECE — An instrument for

recording and acknowledging payment of an indebtedness secured by a mortgage.

SETBACK — The distance a house must be set back from the street in accordance with local zoning rules.

SEVERALTY — A holding by individual right; individual ownership.

SHERIFF'S DEED — An instrument drawn under order of court to convey title to property sold to satisfy a judgment at law.

SITE — Lands made suitable for building purposes by dividing into lots.

SPECIAL WARRANTY DEED — A warranty only against the acts of the grantor himself and all persons claiming through him.

SPECIFIC PERFORMANCE — A remedy in a court of equity compelling the defendant to carry out the terms of a contract.

SUBDIVISION — A tract of land divided into lots suitable for home building purposes.

SUBLETTING — A leasing by a tenant to another.

SUPPLY AND DEMAND, LAW OF — Holds that price varies directly, but not necessarily proportionately, with demand and inversely, but not necessarily proportionately, with supply.

SURVEY — The process by which a parcel of land is measured and its area ascertained.

TANGIBLE PROPERTY — Property that can

be seen and felt. Generally the land, improvements, furnishings and merchandise, including working capital used in carrying on an enterprise.

TAX — A charge laid upon persons or property for public purposes; a forced contribution to meet the public needs of a government.

TAX ABATEMENT — Amount abated; deduction; decrease; rebate, especially of a tax improperly laid.

TAXABLE VALUE — The base upon which taxes are computed under predetermined tax rates. May cover all or any part of the assets represented in tangible and intangible property.

TAX PENALTY — Forfeiture of a sum because of nonpayment of taxes.

TAX SALE — A sale of property, usually at auction, for nonpayment of taxes assessed against it.

TENANCY IN COMMON — Form of estate shared by two or more persons, each of whom is considered as being possessed of the whole part.

TITLE — Evidence of ownership that refers to the quality of the estate.

TITLE COMPANY — A corporation organized for the purpose of issuing or insuring title to real property.

TITLE GUARANTEE POLICY — Title insurance furnished by the owner, provided as an alternative for an abstract of title. Also called

Torrens certificate of title.

TITLE INSURANCE — A policy of insurance that indemnifies the holder for any loss sustained by reason of defects in the title up to the value of the policy.

TORRENS CERTIFICATE — A document, issued by the proper public authority called a "registrar" acting under the provisions of the Torrens Law, indicating the party in whom title resides.

TORRENS SYSTEM — A system of land registration used in some jurisdictions in which the county issues title certificates covering the ownership of land that serve as title insurance.

TRUST DEED — A conveyance of real estate to a third person to be held for the benefit of a beneficiary.

TRUSTEE — One who holds title to property for the benefit of another.

UNIMPROVED — As relating to land, vacant or lacking essential required to serve a useful purpose.

USURY — Charging more than the legal rate of interest for the use of money.

VALUE — Ability to command goods, including money, in exchange; the quantity of goods, including money, which should be commanded in exchange for the item values; utility; desirability. Property value may be broadly defined as the present worth of all of the rights to future benefits arising from ownership.

VENDEE — The purchaser of real estate under an agreement.

VENDOR — The seller of real estate, usually referred to as the party of the first part in an agreement of sale.

WARRANTY DEED — Instrument, in writing, by which a real estate is created or alienated and whereby the fee simple estate is guaranteed by the grantor.

WRIT OF EXECUTION — A legal order that directs an agent of the court (usually a sheriff) to carry out an order of that court.

YIELD — The ratio of the annual net income from the property to the cost or market value of the property.

ZONING — Government regulation of land use; regulation by local government under police power of such matters as height, width and use of buildings and land.

ZONING ORDINANCE — The exercise of police power in a jurisdiction for regulating and controlling the character and use of property.

22

Moving Tips

BEFORE YOU MOVE CONTACT:

☐ **Gas company:** get refund of deposit.

☐ **Electric company:** get refund of deposit.

☐ **Water department:** (if any).

☐ **Newspaper boy:** if prepaid, get refund.

☐ **Milkman:** stop delivery.

☐ **Laundryman:** stop service.

☐ **Bank:** transfer funds and arrange for checking account in the new city.

☐ **Schools:** request the transfer of your children's records.

☐ **Doctor:** ask for referral and transfer records.

☐ **Dentist:** ask for referral and transfer records.

☐ **Optometrist:** ask for referral and transfer records.

☐ **Insurance companies:** life, medical and automobile; notify them of your new location to assure uninterrupted coverage.

☐ **Veternarian:** ask for referral and transfer pet records.

☐ **Post office:** give forwarding address.

☐ **Creditors:** they must know where you're going; otherwise they can't hound you.

☐ **Credit-card companies:** give forwarding address.

☐ **Magazines:** they should be contacted at least a month before you move.

☐ **Friends, relatives and mother-in-law:** give forwarding address.

☐ **Moving company:** get two or three bids.

REMEMBER TO:

☐ Get packing and unpacking help

☐ Check insurance coverage for furnishings in transit.

☐ Empty freezer ahead of time and defrost.

☐ Have appliances ready to be moved.

☐ Get clothes back from cleaners.

☐ Plan for the needs of children and infants.

ON MOVING DAY:

☐ Double check closets, shelves and drawers to be sure they're empty.

☐ Carry valuables and important documents yourself.

☐ Plan for the transportation of pets.

☐ Bring travelers checks.

☐ Be sure a friend or relative knows your route and schedule, including when and where you will stop overnight.

☐ Triple check closets, shelves and drawers to be sure they're still empty.

AT YOUR NEW HOME:

☐ The movers will demand CASH upon delivery.

☐ Have telephone installed.

☐ Contact gas company.

☐ Contact water department (if any).

☐ Check stove at a distance; also hot water heater and furnace.

☐ Register your car within five days after arrival in a different state or you may be fined.

☐ Register your children in school.

☐ If Catholic or Jewish, check your mailbox. Your initial billing from your new priest or rabbi should be there. How he found out God only knows!

Be Sure To Notify Post Office Of Change Of Address

Complete P.O.D. Form 3575. The post office will stop delivery to your address on a designated date and forward future mail to new address. First-Class mail will be forwarded without charge. All second-class newspapers and magazines are forwarded postage due for 90 days if you request it. Early notification to publications advising address change, including new zip code, can avoid postage due costs and also eliminate receiving publications late. If you refuse "postage due", the postmaster at the forwarding post office will discontinue forwarding mail.

23

Forms

CONTRACT TO PURCHASE REAL ESTATE

Date Presented_____

TO THE LEGAL OWNERS:_____

I (We) offer to purchase the property known as: (The parties hereto reserve the right to insert the legal description at a later date.)

_____County of_____State of_____

Lot approximately_____, together with improvements thereon including the following, if any, now on premises: water softner; storm windows and doors; screens; shades; venetian blinds; drapery rods; radiator covers; T.V. antenna; heating; lighting and plumbing fixtures; central cooling; ventilating and air purifying system; awnings; attached mirrors, shelving, cabinets and bookcases; planted vegetation; and all fixtures and fittings appurtenant to or used in the operation of the premises, on the following terms:

This contract to purchase is subject to the terms and conditions of the RIDER(S) attached hereto which is incorporated in and made a part of this contract by reference.

Total purchase price $_____Dollars, payable as follows:

Deposit — Initial earnest money $_____deposited with _____

to be increased to 10% of the purchase price within_____days after acceptance hereof.

Said deposit money shall be returned and this offer shall be void if not accepted by (date and time; or upon presentation)_____

Cash to be paid on delivery of deed $_____

Balance to be paid as follows: The parties hereto understand that it is necessary for the Purchaser to have had made available to him within_____days after the date of acceptance hereof by the Seller, a commitment for a mortgage loan of $_____with interest not to exceed_____% per annum, over a period of_____years, at the reasonable and usual loan commission. Seller shall allow inspections of the premises and furnish any pertinent information required by Purchaser's lending institution in reference to making the loan commitment. If, after the Purchaser has made every reasonable effort to procure such commitment and has been unable to do so, the Purchaser shall serve written notice thereof upon the Seller within the time specified herein for procuring said commitment for a loan, this contract shall thereupon become null and void and all monies paid by Purchaser shall be refunded to him. IN THE EVENT PURCHASER DOES NOT SERVE WRITTEN NOTICE OF HIS FAILURE TO PROCURE A LOAN COMMITMENT UPON THE SELLER WITHIN THE NUMBER OF DAYS AS HEREIN PROVIDED, THEN THIS CONTRACT SHALL CONTINUE IN FULL FORCE AND EFFECT AND THIS PARAGRAPH SHALL BE VOID.

The title closing or escrow pay out shall be at Purchaser's lending institution or at_____

_____ on _____

or before, providing title has been shown good or accepted by Purchaser by conveyance by stamped warranty deed and payment of purchase price.

Title to be conveyed subject to: General real estate taxes for 19____and subsequent years; building, building line and use or occupancy restrictions, conditions or covenants of record; easements and party wall agreements; installments of special assessments falling due after title has been conveyed; special assessments for improvements not yet completed; zoning and building laws or ordinances; roads and highways, if any;

existing leases as follows (to be assigned to Buyer)_____

The following items are to be prorated to date of possession: General real estate taxes (based on most recent ascertainable taxes); interest on encumberences; electric light and gas; water taxes; rents; janitor (including vacation allowance); fuel at market price; and any other usual proratable items.

At or before closing Seller shall furnish to Purchaser one of the following items covering date hereof showing marketable title in Grantor (Seller): (1) A merchantable abstract of title brought down to date hereof, (2) Commitment for title insurance issued by any title insurance company licensed to do business in the state in which the above described property is located, brought down to date hereof, (3) A Torrens certificate accompanied by a Torrens title tax search. If the evidence of title discloses defects Seller shall have 30 additional days from date evidence of title is furnished to cure such defects and notify Purchaser. If Seller is unable to cure such defects Purchaser may, at his election, terminate this contract, or Purchaser may take the title as it then is (with the right to deduct from the purchase price the ascertainable amounts of liens or encumberances) by notifying Seller and tendering performance.

Date of possession by Purchaser shall be not later than 12:00 noon (Date)_____ providing sale has been closed.

Earnest money and this contract shall be held in escrow by_____ for the benefit of the parties hereto. If Purchaser defaults, earnest money shall be forfeited and paid to Seller. At Seller's election such forfeiture may be in full settlement of all damages. If Seller defaults, earnest money, at option of Purchaser, shall be refunded to Purchaser, but such refunding shall not release Seller from the obligation of this contract.

If prior to closing, improvements on said premises shall be destroyed or materially damaged by fire or any other casualty, this contract at the option of Purchaser shall become null and void.

Existing mortgage and other lien indebtedness may be paid at closing out of sale proceeds.

Prior to closing, Seller will furnish an acceptable survey by a licensed land serveyor showing the location of the buildings thereon to be within the lot lines and showing no encroachments of improvements from adjoining properties.

Purchaser may place a mortgage on this property and apply proceeds on purchase.

This contract to purchase when signed by Purchaser(s) and Seller(s) constitutes a binding contract.

Seller warrants to Purchaser that no notice from any city, village or other governmental authority of any dwelling code violation has heretofore been issued and received by the owner or his agent with respect to any dwelling structure on said real estate.

PURCHASER_____ Address_____

PURCHASER_____ _____

This_____ day of_____ 19___, we accept this offer to perform and convey or cause to be conveyed according to the terms of this contract.

SELLER _____ Address_____

SELLER _____ _____

CONTRACT TO PURCHASE REAL ESTATE

Date Presented_____

TO THE LEGAL OWNERS:_____

I (We) offer to purchase the property known as: (The parties hereto reserve the right to insert the legal description at a later date.)

_____County of_____State of_____

Lot approximately_____, together with improvements thereon including the following, if any, now on premises: water softner; storm windows and doors; screens; shades; venetian blinds; drapery rods; radiator covers; T.V. antenna; heating; lighting and plumbing fixtures; central cooling; ventilating and air purifying system; awnings; attached mirrors, shelving, cabinets and bookcases; planted vegetation; and all fixtures and fittings appurtenant to or used in the operation of the premises, on the following terms:

This contract to purchase is subject to the terms and conditions of the RIDER(S) attached hereto which is incorporated in and made a part of this contract by reference.

Total purchase price $_____Dollars, payable as follows:

Deposit — Initial earnest money $_____deposited with _____

to be increased to 10% of the purchase price within_____days after acceptance hereof.

Said deposit money shall be returned and this offer shall be void if not accepted by (date and time; or upon presentation)_____

Cash to be paid on delivery of deed $_____

Balance to be paid as follows: The parties hereto understand that it is necessary for the Purchaser to have had made available to him within_____days after the date of acceptance hereof by the Seller. a commitment for a mortgage loan of $_____with interest not to exceed_____% per annum, over a period of_____years, at the reasonable and usual loan commission. Seller shall allow inspections of the premises and furnish any pertinent information required by Purchaser's lending institution in reference to making the loan commitment. If, after the Purchaser has made every reasonable effort to procure such commitment and has been unable to do so, the Purchaser shall serve written notice thereof upon the Seller within the time specified herein for procuring said commitment for a loan, this contract shall thereupon become null and void and all monies paid by Purchaser shall be refunded to him. IN THE EVENT PURCHASER DOES NOT SERVE WRITTEN NOTICE OF HIS FAILURE TO PROCURE A LOAN COMMITMENT UPON THE SELLER WITHIN THE NUMBER OF DAYS AS HEREIN PROVIDED, THEN THIS CONTRACT SHALL CONTINUE IN FULL FORCE AND EFFECT AND THIS PARAGRAPH SHALL BE VOID.

The title closing or escrow pay out shall be at Purchaser's lending institution or at_____
_____ on _____
or before, providing title has been shown good or accepted by Purchaser by conveyance by stamped warranty deed and payment of purchase price.

Title to be conveyed subject to: General real estate taxes for 19____and subsequent years; building, building line and use or occupancy restrictions, conditions or covenants of record; easements and party wall agreements; installments of special assessments falling due after title has been conveyed; special assessments for improvements not yet completed; zoning and building laws or ordinances; roads and highways, if any;

existing leases as follows (to be assigned to Buyer)_____

The following items are to be prorated to date of possession: General real estate taxes (based on most recent ascertainable taxes); interest on encumberences; electric light and gas; water taxes; rents; janitor (including vacation allowance); fuel at market price; and any other usual proratable items.

At or before closing Seller shall furnish to Purchaser one of the following items covering date hereof showing marketable title in Grantor (Seller): (1) A merchantable abstract of title brought down to date hereof, (2) Commitment for title insurance issued by any title insurance company licensed to do business in the state in which the above described property is located, brought down to date hereof, (3) A Torrens certificate accompanied by a Torrens title tax search. If the evidence of title discloses defects Seller shall have 30 additional days from date evidence of title is furnished to cure such defects and notify Purchaser. If Seller is unable to cure such defects Purchaser may, at his election, terminate this contract, or Purchaser may take the title as it then is (with the right to deduct from the purchase price the ascertainable amounts of liens or encumberances) by notifying Seller and tendering performance.

Date of possession by Purchaser shall be not later than 12:00 noon (Date)_____ providing sale has been closed.

Earnest money and this contract shall be held in escrow by_____ for the benefit of the parties hereto. If Purchaser defaults, earnest money shall be forfeited and paid to Seller. At Seller's election such forfeiture may be in full settlement of all damages. If Seller defaults, earnest money, at option of Purchaser, shall be refunded to Purchaser, but such refunding shall not release Seller from the obligation of this contract.

If prior to closing, improvements on said premises shall be destroyed or materially damaged by fire or any other casualty, this contract at the option of Purchaser shall become null and void.

Existing mortgage and other lien indebtedness may be paid at closing out of sale proceeds.

Prior to closing, Seller will furnish an acceptable survey by a licensed land serveyor showing the location of the buildings thereon to be within the lot lines and showing no encroachments of improvements from adjoining properties.

Purchaser may place a mortgage on this property and apply proceeds on purchase.

This contract to purchase when signed by Purchaser(s) and Seller(s) constitutes a binding contract.

Seller warrants to Purchaser that no notice from any city, village or other governmental authority of any dwelling code violation has heretofore been issued and received by the owner or his agent with respect to any dwelling structure on said real estate.

PURCHASER_____ Address_____

PURCHASER_____ _____

This_____ day of_____ 19___, we accept this offer to perform and convey or cause to be conveyed according to the terms of this contract.

SELLER _____ Address_____

SELLER _____ _____

CONTRACT TO PURCHASE REAL ESTATE

Date Presented_____

TO THE LEGAL OWNERS:_____

I (We) offer to purchase the property known as: (The parties hereto reserve the right to insert the legal description at a later date.)

_____County of_____State of_____

Lot approximately_____., together with improvements thereon including the following, if any, now on premises: water softner; storm windows and doors; screens; shades; venetian blinds; drapery rods; radiator covers; T.V. antenna; heating; lighting and plumbing fixtures; central cooling; ventilating and air purifying system; awnings; attached mirrors, shelving, cabinets and bookcases; planted vegetation; and all fixtures and fittings appurtenant to or used in the operation of the premises, on the following terms:

This contract to purchase is subject to the terms and conditions of the RIDER(S) attached hereto which is incorporated in and made a part of this contract by reference.

Total purchase price $_____Dollars, payable as follows:

Deposit – Initial earnest money $_____deposited with _____

to be increased to 10% of the purchase price within_____days after acceptance hereof.

Said deposit money shall be returned and this offer shall be void if not accepted by (date and time; or upon presentation)_____

Cash to be paid on delivery of deed $_____

Balance to be paid as follows: The parties hereto understand that it is necessary for the Purchaser to have had made available to him within_____days after the date of acceptance hereof by the Seller, a commitment for a mortgage loan of $_____with interest not to exceed_____% per annum, over a period of_____years, at the reasonable and usual loan commission. Seller shall allow inspections of the premises and furnish any pertinent information required by Purchaser's lending institution in reference to making the loan commitment. If, after the Purchaser has made every reasonable effort to procure such commitment and has been unable to do so, the Purchaser shall serve written notice thereof upon the Seller within the time specified herein for procuring said commitment for a loan, this contract shall thereupon become null and void and all monies paid by Purchaser shall be refunded to him. IN THE EVENT PURCHASER DOES NOT SERVE WRITTEN NOTICE OF HIS FAILURE TO PROCURE A LOAN COMMITMENT UPON THE SELLER WITHIN THE NUMBER OF DAYS AS HEREIN PROVIDED, THEN THIS CONTRACT SHALL CONTINUE FULL FORCE AND EFFECT AND THIS PARAGRAPH SHALL BE VOID.

The title closing or escrow pay out shall be at Purchaser's lending institution or at_____
_____ on _____
or before, providing title has been shown good or accepted by Purchaser by conveyance by stamped warranty deed and payment of purchase price.

Title to be conveyed subject to: General real estate taxes for 19____and subsequent years; building, building line and use or occupancy restrictions, conditions or covenants of record; easements and party wall agreements; installments of special assessments falling due after title has been conveyed; special assessments for improvements not yet completed; zoning and building laws or ordinances; roads and highways, if any;

existing leases as follows (to be assigned to Buyer)_____

The following items are to be prorated to date of possession: General real estate taxes (based on most recent ascertainable taxes); interest on encumberences; electric light and gas; water taxes; rents; janitor (including vacation allowance); fuel at market price; and any other usual proratable items.

At or before closing Seller shall furnish to Purchaser one of the following items covering date hereof showing marketable title in Grantor (Seller): (1) A merchantable abstract of title brought down to date hereof, (2) Commitment for title insurance issued by any title insurance company licensed to do business in the state in which the above described property is located, brought down to date hereof, (3) A Torrens certificate accompanied by a Torrens title tax search. If the evidence of title discloses defects Seller shall have 30 additional days from date evidence of title is furnished to cure such defects and notify Purchaser. If Seller is unable to cure such defects Purchaser may, at his election, terminate this contract, or Purchaser may take the title as it then is (with the right to deduct from the purchase price the ascertainable amounts of liens or encumberances) by notifying Seller and tendering performance.

Date of possession by Purchaser shall be not later than 12:00 noon (Date)_____ providing sale has been closed.

Earnest money and this contract shall be held in escrow by_____ for the benefit of the parties hereto. If Purchaser defaults, earnest money shall be forfeited and paid to Seller. At Seller's election such forfeiture may be in full settlement of all damages. If Seller defaults, earnest money, at option of Purchaser, shall be refunded to Purchaser, but such refunding shall not release Seller from the obligation of this contract.

If prior to closing, improvements on said premises shall be destroyed or materially damaged by fire or any other casualty, this contract at the option of Purchaser shall become null and void.

Existing mortgage and other lien indebtedness may be paid at closing out of sale proceeds.

Prior to closing, Seller will furnish an acceptable survey by a licensed land serveyor showing the location of the buildings thereon to be within the lot lines and showing no encroachments of improvements from adjoining properties.

Purchaser may place a mortgage on this property and apply proceeds on purchase.

This contract to purchase when signed by Purchaser(s) and Seller(s) constitutes a binding contract.

Seller warrants to Purchaser that no notice from any city, village or other governmental authority of any dwelling code violation has heretofore been issued and received by the owner or his agent with respect to any dwelling structure on said real estate.

PURCHASER_____ Address_____

PURCHASER_____ _____

This_____ day of_____ 19___, we accept this offer to perform and convey or cause to be conveyed according to the terms of this contract.

SELLER _____ Address_____

SELLER _____ _____

CONTRACT TO PURCHASE REAL ESTATE

Date Presented_____

TO THE LEGAL OWNERS:_____

I (We) offer to purchase the property known as: (The parties hereto reserve the right to insert the legal description at a later date.)

_____County of_____State of_____

Lot approximately_____, together with improvements thereon including the following, if any, now on premises: water softner; storm windows and doors; screens; shades; venetian blinds; drapery rods; radiator covers; T.V. antenna; heating; lighting and plumbing fixtures; central cooling; ventilating and air purifying system; awnings; attached mirrors, shelving, cabinets and bookcases; planted vegetation; and all fixtures and fittings appurtenant to or used in the operation of the premises, on the following terms:

This contract to purchase is subject to the terms and conditions of the RIDER(S) attached hereto which is incorporated in and made a part of this contract by reference.

Total purchase price $_____Dollars, payable as follows:

Deposit — Initial earnest money $_____deposited with _____

to be increased to 10% of the purchase price within_____days after acceptance hereof.

Said deposit money shall be returned and this offer shall be void if not accepted by (date and time; or upon presentation)_____

Cash to be paid on delivery of deed $_____

Balance to be paid as follows: The parties hereto understand that it is necessary for the Purchaser to have had made available to him within_____days after the date of acceptance hereof by the Seller, a commitment for a mortgage loan of $_____with interest not to exceed_____% per annum, over a period of_____years, at the reasonable and usual loan commission. Seller shall allow inspections of the premises and furnish any pertinent information required by Purchaser's lending institution in reference to making the loan commitment. If, after the Purchaser has made every reasonable effort to procure such commitment and has been unable to do so, the Purchaser shall serve written notice thereof upon the Seller within the time specified herein for procuring said commitment for a loan, this contract shall thereupon become null and void and all monies paid by Purchaser shall be refunded to him. IN THE EVENT PURCHASER DOES NOT SERVE WRITTEN NOTICE OF HIS FAILURE TO PROCURE A LOAN COMMITMENT UPON THE SELLER WITHIN THE NUMBER OF DAYS AS HEREIN PROVIDED, THEN THIS CONTRACT SHALL CONTINUE IN FULL FORCE AND EFFECT AND THIS PARAGRAPH SHALL BE VOID.

The title closing or escrow pay out shall be at Purchaser's lending institution or at_____ _____ on _____

or before, providing title has been shown good or accepted by Purchaser by conveyance by stamped warranty deed and payment of purchase price.

Title to be conveyed subject to: General real estate taxes for 19____and subsequent years; building, building line and use or occupancy restrictions, conditions or covenants of record; easements and party wall agreements; installments of special assessments falling due after title has been conveyed; special assessments for improvements not yet completed; zoning and building laws or ordinances; roads and highways, if any;

existing leases as follows (to be assigned to Buyer)_____

The following items are to be prorated to date of possession: General real estate taxes (based on most recent ascertainable taxes); interest on encumberences; electric light and gas; water taxes; rents; janitor (including vacation allowance); fuel at market price; and any other usual proratable items.

At or before closing Seller shall furnish to Purchaser one of the following items covering date hereof showing marketable title in Grantor (Seller): (1) A merchantable abstract of title brought down to date hereof, (2) Commitment for title insurance issued by any title insurance company licensed to do business in the state in which the above described property is located, brought down to date hereof, (3) A Torrens certificate accompanied by a Torrens title tax search. If the evidence of title discloses defects Seller shall have 30 additional days from date evidence of title is furnished to cure such defects and notify Purchaser. If Seller is unable to cure such defects Purchaser may, at his election, terminate this contract, or Purchaser may take the title as it then is (with the right to deduct from the purchase price the ascertainable amounts of liens or encumberances) by notifying Seller and tendering performance.

Date of possession by Purchaser shall be not later than 12:00 noon (Date)_____ providing sale has been closed.

Earnest money and this contract shall be held in escrow by_____ for the benefit of the parties hereto. If Purchaser defaults, earnest money shall be forfeited and paid to Seller. At Seller's election such forfeiture may be in full settlement of all damages. If Seller defaults, earnest money, at option of Purchaser, shall be refunded to Purchaser, but such refunding shall not release Seller from the obligation of this contract.

If prior to closing, improvements on said premises shall be destroyed or materially damaged by fire or any other casualty, this contract at the option of Purchaser shall become null and void.

Existing mortgage and other lien indebtedness may be paid at closing out of sale proceeds.

Prior to closing, Seller will furnish an acceptable survey by a licensed land serveyor showing the location of the buildings thereon to be within the lot lines and showing no encroachments of improvements from adjoining properties.

Purchaser may place a mortgage on this property and apply proceeds on purchase.

This contract to purchase when signed by Purchaser(s) and Seller(s) constitutes a binding contract.

Seller warrants to Purchaser that no notice from any city, village or other governmental authority of any dwelling code violation has heretofore been issued and received by the owner or his agent with respect to any dwelling structure on said real estate.

PURCHASER_____ Address_____

PURCHASER_____ _____

This_____ day of_____ 19___, we accept this offer to perform and convey or cause to be conveyed according to the terms of this contract.

SELLER _____ Address_____

SELLER _____ _____

PERSONAL PROPERTY RIDER

RE: Property at _____

It is understood and agreed between the SELLERS and the PURCHASERS of the aforementioned property that the following items, presently on the premises and in use, are to be included in the purchase price of $_____ .   _____

_____

_____

_____

_____

_____

_____

_____

_____

_____

_____

_____

_____

_____

_____

_____

Date _____ Purchaser _____

                                   Purchaser _____

Date _____ Seller _____

                                   Seller _____

PERSONAL PROPERTY RIDER

RE: Property at _____

It is understood and agreed between the SELLERS and the PURCHASERS of the aforementioned property that the following items, presently on the premises and in use, are to be included in the purchase price of $_____.   _____

_____

_____

_____

_____

_____

_____

_____

_____

_____

_____

_____

_____

_____

_____

Date _____ Purchaser _____

                               Purchaser _____

Date _____ Seller _____

                               Seller _____

PERSONAL PROPERTY RIDER

RE: Property at _____

It is understood and agreed between the SELLERS and the PURCHASERS of the aforementioned property that the following items, presently on the premises and in use, are to be included in the purchase price of $_____ .   _____

_____

_____

_____

_____

_____

_____

_____

_____

_____

_____

_____

_____

_____

_____

_____

_____

Date _____ Purchaser _____

                                              Purchaser _____

Date _____ Seller _____

                                              Seller _____

PERSONAL PROPERTY RIDER

RE: Property at _____

It is understood and agreed between the SELLERS and the PURCHASERS of the aforementioned property that the following items, presently on the premises and in use, are to be included in the purchase price of $_____ . _____

_____

_____

_____

_____

_____

_____

_____

_____

_____

_____

_____

_____

_____

_____

_____

Date _____ Purchaser _____

Purchaser _____

Date _____ Seller _____

Seller _____

CONTRACT CONTINGENT ON
SPOUSE'S APPROVAL

THIS RIDER IS ATTACHED TO AND MADE PART OF THE REAL ESTATE SALES CONTRACT

DATED: _____ , 19____, between _____ and

_____ , as Purchasers, and_____ and

_____ , as Sellers.

    This contract to purchase is subject to the approval of the property by Buyer's spouse within (max. 48 hours)_____hours of (date of contract)_____time (of contract)_____a.m./p.m. o'clock. In the event the spouse does not approve of the property, written notice as provided herein shall be given to the Seller or his agent within the time specified for said spouse's approval and thereupon this contract shall become null and void and all monies paid by the Buyer shall be refunded to him. In the event the Buyer does not serve said notice upon Seller or his agent that the Buyer's spouse does not approve of said property then this contract shall continue in full force and effect and this condition shall be void.

Date_____

Accepted:

Purchaser _____

Purchaser _____

Seller _____

Seller _____

CONTRACT CONTINGENT ON
SPOUSE'S APPROVAL

THIS RIDER IS ATTACHED TO AND MADE PART OF THE REAL ESTATE SALES CONTRACT

DATED: _____, 19____, between _____ and

_____, as Purchasers, and_____ and

_____, as Sellers.

This contract to purchase is subject to the approval of the property by Buyer's spouse within (max. 48 hours)_____hours of (date of contract)_____time (of contract)_____a.m./p.m. o'clock. In the event the spouse does not approve of the property, written notice as provided herein shall be given to the Seller or his agent within the time specified for said spouse's approval and thereupon this contract shall become null and void and all monies paid by the Buyer shall be refunded to him. In the event the Buyer does not serve said notice upon Seller or his agent that the Buyer's spouse does not approve of said property then this contract shall continue in full force and effect and this condition shall be void.

Date_____

Accepted:

Purchaser _____

Purchaser _____

Seller _____

Seller _____

CONTRACT CONTINGENT ON
SPOUSE'S APPROVAL

THIS RIDER IS ATTACHED TO AND MADE PART OF THE REAL ESTATE SALES CONTRACT

DATED: _____, 19___, between _____ and

_____, as Purchasers, and _____ and

_____, as Sellers.

This contract to purchase is subject to the approval of the property by Buyer's spouse within (max. 48 hours)_____hours of (date of contract)_____time (of contract)_____a.m./p.m. o'clock. In the event the spouse does not approve of the property, written notice as provided herein shall be given to the Seller or his agent within the time specified for said spouse's approval and thereupon this contract shall become null and void and all monies paid by the Buyer shall be refunded to him. In the event the Buyer does not serve said notice upon Seller or his agent that the Buyer's spouse does not approve of said property then this contract shall continue in full force and effect and this condition shall be void.

Date_____

Accepted:

Purchaser _____

Purchaser _____

Seller _____

Seller _____

CONTRACT CONTINGENT ON
SPOUSE'S APPROVAL

THIS RIDER IS ATTACHED TO AND MADE PART OF THE REAL ESTATE SALES CONTRACT

DATED: _____, 19___, between _____ and

_____, as Purchasers, and _____ and

_____, as Sellers.

This contract to purchase is subject to the approval of the property by Buyer's spouse within (max. 48 hours)_____hours of (date of contract)_____ time (of contract)_____a.m./p.m. o'clock. In the event the spouse does not approve of the property, written notice as provided herein shall be given to the Seller or his agent within the time specified for said spouse's approval and thereupon this contract shall become null and void and all monies paid by the Buyer shall be refunded to him. In the event the Buyer does not serve said notice upon Seller or his agent that the Buyer's spouse does not approve of said property then this contract shall continue in full force and effect and this condition shall be void.

Date_____

Accepted:

Purchaser _____

Purchaser _____

Seller _____

Seller _____

VA APPRAISAL CONTINGENCY

THIS RIDER IS ATTACHED TO AND MADE PART OF THE REAL ESTATE SALES CONTRACT

DATED: _____ , 19 ____ , between _____ and

_____ , as Purchasers, and _____ and

_____ , as Sellers.

AMENDMENT TO VA CONTRACT

"It is expressly agreed that, notwithstanding any other provision of this contract, the Purchaser shall not incur any penalty by forfeiture of earnest money or otherwise or be obligated to complete the purchase of the property described herein, if the contract purchase price or cost exceeds the reasonable value of the property established by the Veterans Administration. The Purchaser shall, however, have the privilege and option of proceeding with the consummation of this contract without regard to the amount of the reasonable value established by the Veterans Administration."

Date _____

Veteran Purchaser _____

Purchaser _____

Seller _____

Seller _____

VA APPRAISAL CONTINGENCY

THIS RIDER IS ATTACHED TO AND MADE PART OF THE REAL ESTATE SALES CONTRACT

DATED: _____ , 19 ____ , between _____ and

_____ , as Purchasers, and _____ and

_____ , as Sellers.

AMENDMENT TO VA CONTRACT

"It is expressly agreed that, notwithstanding any other provision of this contract, the Purchaser shall not incur any penalty by forfeiture of earnest money or otherwise or be obligated to complete the purchase of the property described herein, if the contract purchase price or cost exceeds the reasonable value of the property established by the Veterans Administration. The Purchaser shall, however, have the privilege and option of proceeding with the consummation of this contract without regard to the amount of the reasonable value established by the Veterans Administration."

Date _____

Veteran Purchaser _____

Purchaser _____

Seller _____

Seller _____

VA APPRAISAL CONTINGENCY

THIS RIDER IS ATTACHED TO AND MADE PART OF THE REAL ESTATE SALES CONTRACT

DATED: _____ , 19 ___ , between _____ and

_____ , as Purchasers, and _____ and

_____ , as Sellers.

AMENDMENT TO VA CONTRACT

"It is expressly agreed that, notwithstanding any other provision of this contract, the Purchaser shall not incur any penalty by forfeiture of earnest money or otherwise or be obligated to complete the purchase of the property described herein, if the contract purchase price or cost exceeds the reasonable value of the property established by the Veterans Administration. The Purchaser shall, however, have the privilege and option of proceeding with the consummation of this contract without regard to the amount of the reasonable value established by the Veterans Administration."

Date _____

Veteran Purchaser _____

Purchaser _____

Seller _____

Seller _____

VA APPRAISAL CONTINGENCY

THIS RIDER IS ATTACHED TO AND MADE PART OF THE REAL ESTATE SALES CONTRACT

DATED: _____ , 19 ____ , between _____ and

_____ , as Purchasers, and _____ and

_____ , as Sellers.

AMENDMENT TO VA CONTRACT

"It is expressly agreed that, notwithstanding any other provision of this contract, the Purchaser shall not incur any penalty by forfeiture of earnest money or otherwise or be obligated to complete the purchase of the property described herein, if the contract purchase price or cost exceeds the reasonable value of the property established by the Veterans Administration. The Purchaser shall, however, have the privilege and option of proceeding with the consummation of this contract without regard to the amount of the reasonable value established by the Veterans Administration."

Date _____

Veteran Purchaser _____

Purchaser _____

Seller _____

Seller _____

FHA APPRAISAL CONTINGENCY

THIS RIDER IS ATTACHED TO AND MADE PART OF THE REAL ESTATE SALES CONTRACT

DATED: _____, 19___, between _____ and

_____, as Purchasers, and _____ and

_____, as Sellers.

"It is expressly agreed that, notwithstanding any other provisions of this contract, the purchaser shall not be obligated to complete the purchase of the property described herein or to incur any penalty by forfeiture of earnest money deposits or otherwise unless the seller has delivered to the purchaser a written statement issued by the Federal Housing Commissioner setting forth the appraised value of the property for mortgage insurance purposes of not less than $_____, which statement the seller hereby agrees to deliver to the purchaser promptly after such appraised value statement is made available to the seller."

"The purchaser shall, however, have the privilege and option of proceeding with the consummation of this contract without regard to the amount of the appraised valuation made by the Federal Housing Commissioner."

Date _____   Purchaser _____

                                  Purchaser _____

Date _____   Seller _____

                                  Seller _____

FHA APPRAISAL CONTINGENCY

THIS RIDER IS ATTACHED TO AND MADE PART OF THE REAL ESTATE SALES CONTRACT

DATED: _____, 19___, between _____ and

_____, as Purchasers, and _____ and

_____, as Sellers.

"It is expressly agreed that, notwithstanding any other provisions of this contract, the purchaser shall not be obligated to complete the purchase of the property described herein or to incur any penalty by forfeiture of earnest money deposits or otherwise unless the seller has delivered to the purchaser a written statement issued by the Federal Housing Commissioner setting forth the appraised value of the property for mortgage insurance purposes of not less than $_____, which statement the seller hereby agrees to deliver to the purchaser promptly after such appraised value statement is made available to the seller."

"The purchaser shall, however, have the privilege and option of proceeding with the consummation of this contract without regard to the amount of the appraised valuation made by the Federal Housing Commissioner."

Date _____ Purchaser _____

Purchaser _____

Date _____ Seller _____

Seller _____

FHA APPRAISAL CONTINGENCY

THIS RIDER IS ATTACHED TO AND MADE PART OF THE REAL ESTATE SALES CONTRACT

DATED:_____, 19___, between_____ and

_____, as Purchasers, and_____ and

_____, as Sellers.

"It is expressly agreed that, notwithstanding any other provisions of this contract, the purchaser shall not be obligated to complete the purchase of the property described herein or to incur any penalty by forfeiture of earnest money deposits or otherwise unless the seller has delivered to the purchaser a written statement issued by the Federal Housing Commissioner setting forth the appraised value of the property for mortgage insurance purposes of not less than $_____, which statement the seller hereby agrees to deliver to the purchaser promptly after such appraised value statement is made available to the seller."

"The purchaser shall, however, have the privilege and option of proceeding with the consummation of this contract without regard to the amount of the appraised valuation made by the Federal Housing Commissioner."

Date_____ Purchaser_____

Purchaser_____

Date_____ Seller_____

Seller_____

FHA APPRAISAL CONTINGENCY

THIS RIDER IS ATTACHED TO AND MADE PART OF THE REAL ESTATE SALES CONTRACT

DATED: _____, 19___, between _____ and

_____, as Purchasers, and _____ and

_____, as Sellers.

"It is expressly agreed that, notwithstanding any other provisions of this contract, the purchaser shall not be obligated to complete the purchase of the property described herein or to incur any penalty by forfeiture of earnest money deposits or otherwise unless the seller has delivered to the purchaser a written statement issued by the Federal Housing Commissioner setting forth the appraised value of the property for mortgage insurance purposes of not less than $_____, which statement the seller hereby agrees to deliver to the purchaser promptly after such appraised value statement is made available to the seller."

"The purchaser shall, however, have the privilege and option of proceeding with the consummation of this contract without regard to the amount of the appraised valuation made by the Federal Housing Commissioner."

Date _____ Purchaser _____

                                 Purchaser _____

Date _____ Seller _____

                                 Seller _____

CONTRACT CONTINGENT ON
BUYER'S ATTORNEY'S APPROVAL

THIS RIDER IS ATTACHED TO AND MADE PART OF THE REAL ESTATE SALES CONTRACT

DATED:_____, 19___, between _____ and

_____, as Purchasers, and _____ and

_____, as Sellers.

This contract to purchase is subject to the approval of the Buyer's attorney as it pertains to legal matters only, with (max. 48 hours)_____hours of (date of contract)_____time (of contract)_____a.m./p.m. o'clock. In the absence of written notice within the time specified herein, this provision shall be deemed waived by all parties hereto and this contract shall be in full force and effect.

Date _____

Accepted:

Purchaser _____

Purchaser _____

Seller _____

Seller _____

CONTRACT CONTINGENT ON
BUYER'S ATTORNEY'S APPROVAL

THIS RIDER IS ATTACHED TO AND MADE PART OF THE REAL ESTATE SALES CONTRACT

DATED:_____ , 19___, between _____ and

_____ , as Purchasers, and _____ and

_____ , as Sellers.

This contract to purchase is subject to the approval of the Buyer's attorney as it pertains to legal matters only, with (max. 48 hours)_____hours of (date of contract)_____time (of contract)_____a.m./p.m. o'clock. In the absence of written notice within the time specified herein, this provision shall be deemed waived by all parties hereto and this contract shall be in full force and effect.

Date _____

Accepted:

Purchaser _____

Purchaser _____

Seller _____

Seller _____

CONTRACT CONTINGENT ON
BUYER'S ATTORNEY'S APPROVAL

THIS RIDER IS ATTACHED TO AND MADE PART OF THE REAL ESTATE SALES CONTRACT

DATED:_____ , 19___, between _____ and

_____ , as Purchasers, and _____ and

_____ , as Sellers.

This contract to purchase is subject to the approval of the Buyer's attorney as it pertains to legal matters only, with (max. 48 hours)_____hours of (date of contract)_____time (of contract)_____a.m./p.m. o'clock. In the absence of written notice within the time specified herein, this provision shall be deemed waived by all parties hereto and this contract shall be in full force and effect.

Date _____

Accepted:

Purchaser _____

Purchaser _____

Seller _____

Seller _____

CONTRACT CONTINGENT ON
BUYER'S ATTORNEY'S APPROVAL

THIS RIDER IS ATTACHED TO AND MADE PART OF THE REAL ESTATE SALES CONTRACT

DATED:_____ , 19___, between _____ and

_____ , as Purchasers, and _____ and

_____ , as Sellers.

This contract to purchase is subject to the approval of the Buyer's attorney as it pertains to legal matters only, with (max. 48 hours)_____hours of (date of contract)_____time (of contract)_____a.m./p.m. o'clock. In the absence of written notice within the time specified herein, this provision shall be deemed waived by all parties hereto and this contract shall be in full force and effect.

Date _____

Accepted:

Purchaser_____

Purchaser_____

Seller _____

Seller _____

CONTRACT CONTINGENT ON
SELLER'S ATTORNEY'S APPROVAL

THIS RIDER IS ATTACHED TO AND MADE PART OF THE REAL ESTATE SALES CONTRACT

DATED: _____, 19___, between _____ and

_____, as Purchasers, and _____ and

_____, as Sellers.

This contract to purchase is subject to the approval of the Seller's attorney within (max. 48 hours)_____hours of (date of contract)_____time (of contract)_____a.m./p.m. o'clock. In the absence of written notice within the time specified herein, this provision shall be deemed waived by all parties hereto and this contract shall be in full force and effect.

Date _____

Accepted:

Purchaser _____

Purchaser _____

Seller _____

Seller _____

CONTRACT CONTINGENT ON
SELLER'S ATTORNEY'S APPROVAL

THIS RIDER IS ATTACHED TO AND MADE PART OF THE REAL ESTATE SALES CONTRACT

DATED: _____, 19___, between _____ and

_____, as Purchasers, and _____ and

_____, as Sellers.

This contract to purchase is subject to the approval of the Seller's attorney within (max. 48 hours)_____hours of (date of contract)_____time (of contract)_____a.m./p.m. o'clock. In the absence of written notice within the time specified herein, this provision shall be deemed waived by all parties hereto and this contract shall be in full force and effect.

Date _____

Accepted:

Purchaser _____

Purchaser _____

Seller _____

Seller _____

CONTRACT CONTINGENT ON
SELLER'S ATTORNEY'S APPROVAL

THIS RIDER IS ATTACHED TO AND MADE PART OF THE REAL ESTATE SALES CONTRACT

DATED: _____, 19___, between _____ and

_____, as Purchasers, and _____ and

_____, as Sellers.

This contract to purchase is subject to the approval of the Seller's attorney within (max. 48 hours)_____hours of (date of contract)_____time (of contract)_____a.m./p.m. o'clock. In the absence of written notice within the time specified herein, this provision shall be deemed waived by all parties hereto and this contract shall be in full force and effect.

Date _____

Accepted:

Purchaser _____

Purchaser _____

Seller _____

Seller _____

CONTRACT CONTINGENT ON
SELLER'S ATTORNEY'S APPROVAL

THIS RIDER IS ATTACHED TO AND MADE PART OF THE REAL ESTATE SALES CONTRACT

DATED:_____, 19___, between _____ and

_____, as Purchasers, and_____ and

_____, as Sellers.

This contract to purchase is subject to the approval of the Seller's attorney within (max. 48 hours)_____hours of (date of contract)_____time (of contract)_____a.m./p.m. o'clock. In the absence of written notice within the time specified herein, this provision shall be deemed waived by all parties hereto and this contract shall be in full force and effect.

Date _____

Accepted:

Purchaser _____

Purchaser _____

Seller _____

Seller _____

CONTRACT CONTINGENT ON THE
SALE OF BUYER'S PRESENT HOME

THIS RIDER IS ATTACHED TO AND MADE PART OF THE REAL ESTATE SALES CONTRACT

DATED: _____, 19____ between _____ and

_____, as Purchasers, and _____ and

_____, as Sellers.

This contract to purchase is subject to the sale of the Buyer's present home located at:_____

_____ County_____State_____

on or before (date)_____19___.

        If said property is not sold within the time specified the Buyer shall give the Seller or his agent written notice as provided herein of such failure within the time allowed for the sale whereupon this contract shall become null and void and all monies paid by the Buyer shall be refunded. In the event the Buyer does not serve notice upon the Seller or his agent as herein provided then this contract shall continue in full force and effect and this condition shall be void.

        Seller shall have the right to cancel this contract by giving the Buyer herein 24 hours written notice that the Seller has received a bonafide contract to purchase the property herein non-contingent on the sale of other real estate, on like or better terms than those set forth herein, if within said 24 hour period Buyer does not delete this contingency in writing thereby agreeing to complete this purchase regardless of whether or not Buyer's home is sold. If not so removed, this contract shall become null and void and all monies paid by Buyer shall be refunded.

Date_____

Accepted:

Purchaser _____

Purchaser _____

Seller_____

Seller_____

CONTRACT CONTINGENT ON THE SALE OF BUYER'S PRESENT HOME

THIS RIDER IS ATTACHED TO AND MADE PART OF THE REAL ESTATE SALES CONTRACT

DATED: _____, 19____ between _____ and

_____, as Purchasers, and _____ and

_____, as Sellers.

This contract to purchase is subject to the sale of the Buyer's present home located at:_____

_____ County _____ State _____

on or before (date)_____ 19____.

        If said property is not sold within the time specified the Buyer shall give the Seller or his agent written notice as provided herein of such failure within the time allowed for the sale whereupon this contract shall become null and void and all monies paid by the Buyer shall be refunded. In the event the Buyer does not serve notice upon the Seller or his agent as herein provided then this contract shall continue in full force and effect and this condition shall be void.

        Seller shall have the right to cancel this contract by giving the Buyer herein 24 hours written notice that the Seller has received a bonafide contract to purchase the property herein non-contingent on the sale of other real estate, on like or better terms than those set forth herein, if within said 24 hour period Buyer does not delete this contingency in writing thereby agreeing to complete this purchase regardless of whether or not Buyer's home is sold. If not so removed, this contract shall become null and void and all monies paid by Buyer shall be refunded.

Date _____

Accepted:

Purchaser _____

Purchaser _____

Seller _____

Seller _____

CONTRACT CONTINGENT ON THE
SALE OF BUYER'S PRESENT HOME

THIS RIDER IS ATTACHED TO AND MADE PART OF THE REAL ESTATE SALES CONTRACT

DATED: _____, 19____ between _____ and

_____, as Purchasers, and _____ and

_____, as Sellers.

This contract to purchase is subject to the sale of the Buyer's present home located at:_____

_____ County _____ State _____

on or before (date)_____ 19____.

If said property is not sold within the time specified the Buyer shall give the Seller or his agent written notice as provided herein of such failure within the time allowed for the sale whereupon this contract shall become null and void and all monies paid by the Buyer shall be refunded. In the event the Buyer does not serve notice upon the Seller or his agent as herein provided then this contract shall continue in full force and effect and this condition shall be void.

Seller shall have the right to cancel this contract by giving the Buyer herein 24 hours written notice that the Seller has received a bonafide contract to purchase the property herein non-contingent on the sale of other real estate, on like or better terms than those set forth herein, if within said 24 hour period Buyer does not delete this contingency in writing thereby agreeing to complete this purchase regardless of whether or not Buyer's home is sold. If not so removed, this contract shall become null and void and all monies paid by Buyer shall be refunded.

Date _____

Accepted:

Purchaser _____

Purchaser _____

Seller _____

Seller _____

CONTRACT CONTINGENT ON THE SALE OF BUYER'S PRESENT HOME

THIS RIDER IS ATTACHED TO AND MADE PART OF THE REAL ESTATE SALES CONTRACT

DATED: _____, 19___ between _____ and

_____, as Purchasers, and _____ and

_____, as Sellers.

This contract to purchase is subject to the sale of the Buyer's present home located at:_____

_____ County _____ State _____

on or before (date)_____ 19___.

If said property is not sold within the time specified the Buyer shall give the Seller or his agent written notice as provided herein of such failure within the time allowed for the sale whereupon this contract shall become null and void and all monies paid by the Buyer shall be refunded. In the event the Buyer does not serve notice upon the Seller or his agent as herein provided then this contract shall continue in full force and effect and this condition shall be void.

Seller shall have the right to cancel this contract by giving the Buyer herein 24 hours written notice that the Seller has received a bonafide contract to purchase the property herein non-contingent on the sale of other real estate, on like or better terms than those set forth herein, if within said 24 hour period Buyer does not delete this contingency in writing thereby agreeing to complete this purchase regardless of whether or not Buyer's home is sold. If not so removed, this contract shall become null and void and all monies paid by Buyer shall be refunded.

Date _____

Accepted:

Purchaser _____

Purchaser _____

Seller _____

Seller _____

CONFIDENTIAL BUYER QUALIFICATION FORM

(Please Print)

Name _____ Age _____

Spouse _____ Age _____

Address _____ City _____ Zip _____

Number of Dependents _____ Ages _____

Phone { Home _____

Office _____

Financing Desired: VA ☐ FHA ☐ CONV. ☐ OTHER _____

Preferred Down Payment $ _____ Maximum, if needed $ _____

Preferred Monthly Payment $ _____ Maximum, if needed $ _____

Husband	**Wife**
Employer _____	Employer _____
Address _____	Address _____
Position _____ How Long _____ yrs.	Position _____ How Long _____ yrs.
Average Monthly Income $ _____	Average Monthly Income $ _____

Total Earnings before taxes for last three years:

19 _____ $ _____   19 _____ $ _____   19 _____ $ _____

	Monthly	Yearly
Husband's Income	$ _____	$ _____
Other Income (explain)	$ _____	$ _____
Wife's Income	$ _____	$ _____
Other Income (explain)	$ _____	$ _____
Totals.	$ _____	$ _____

Assets		Liabilities	Monthly Payment	Unpaid Balance
Cash.	$ _____	Auto.	$ _____	$ _____
Stocks, Bonds, etc.	$ _____	Real Estate.	$ _____	$ _____
Life Insurance (Cash Value)	$ _____	Loans.	$ _____	$ _____
Real Estate	$ _____	Other	$ _____	$ _____
Other	$ _____	Other	$ _____	$ _____
Total	$ _____	Total	$ _____	$ _____

Have you ever been involved in a Bankruptcy, Wage Garnishment, Mortgage Foreclosure, Receivership, or Judgement proceedings, or any other credit problems during the past ten years? ☐ Yes ☐ No If yes, please explain on the reverse side.

I hereby certify that the foregoing information is true and accurate to the best of my knowledge and belief.

Date _____   _____

Signature of Buyer

CONFIDENTIAL BUYER QUALIFICATION FORM
(Please Print)

Name _____ Age _____

Spouse _____ Age _____

Address _____ City _____ Zip _____

Number of Dependents _____ Ages _____

Phone { Home _____
       { Office _____

Financing Desired: VA ☐ FHA ☐ CONV. ☐ OTHER _____

Preferred Down Payment $ _____ Maximum, if needed $ _____

Preferred Monthly Payment $ _____ Maximum, if needed $ _____

Husband	Wife
Employer _____	Employer _____
Address _____	Address _____
Position _____ How Long _____ yrs.	Position _____ How Long _____ yrs.
Average Monthly Income $ _____	Average Monthly Income $ _____

Total Earnings before taxes for last three years:

19 _____ $ _____   19 _____ $ _____   19 _____ $ _____

	Monthly	Yearly
Husband's Income	$ _____	$ _____
Other Income (explain)	$ _____	$ _____
Wife's Income	$ _____	$ _____
Other Income (explain)	$ _____	$ _____
Totals.	$ _____	$ _____

Assets		Liabilities	Monthly Payment	Unpaid Balance
Cash.	$ _____	Auto.	$ _____	$ _____
Stocks, Bonds, etc.	$ _____	Real Estate.	$ _____	$ _____
Life Insurance (Cash Value)	$ _____	Loans.	$ _____	$ _____
Real Estate	$ _____	Other	$ _____	$ _____
Other.	$ _____	Other	$ _____	$ _____
Total	$ _____	Total	$ _____	$ _____

Have you ever been involved in a Bankruptcy, Wage Garnishment, Mortgage Foreclosure, Receivership, or Judgement proceedings, or any other credit problems during the past ten years? ☐ Yes ☐ No If yes, please explain on the reverse side.

I hereby certify that the foregoing information is true and accurate to the best of my knowledge and belief.

Date _____   _____
                                Signature of Buyer

CONFIDENTIAL BUYER QUALIFICATION FORM

(Please Print)

Name _____ Age _____

Spouse _____ Age _____

Address _____ City _____ Zip _____

Number of Dependents _____ Ages _____

Phone { Home _____
       { Office _____

Financing Desired: VA ☐   FHA ☐   CONV. ☐   OTHER _____

Preferred Down Payment $ _____ Maximum, if needed $ _____

Preferred Monthly Payment $ _____ Maximum, if needed $ _____

Husband	Wife
Employer _____	Employer _____
Address _____	Address _____
Position _____ How Long _____ yrs.	Position _____ How Long _____ yrs.
Average Monthly Income $ _____	Average Monthly Income $ _____

Total Earnings before taxes for last three years:

19 _____ $ _____   19 _____ $ _____   19 _____ $ _____

	Monthly	Yearly
Husband's Income	$ _____	$ _____
Other Income (explain)	$ _____	$ _____
Wife's Income	$ _____	$ _____
Other Income (explain)	$ _____	$ _____
Totals.	$ _____	$ _____

Assets	Liabilities	Monthly Payment	Unpaid Balance
Cash. . . . . $ _____	Auto. . . . . $ _____		$ _____
Stocks, Bonds, etc. . . . . $ _____	Real Estate. . . . . $ _____		$ _____
Life Insurance (Cash Value) . . . $ _____	Loans. . . . . $ _____		$ _____
Real Estate . . . . $ _____	Other . . . . $ _____		$ _____
Other. . . . . $ _____	Other . . . . $ _____		$ _____
Total . . . . $ _____	Total . . . . $ _____		$ _____

Have you ever been involved in a Bankruptcy, Wage Garnishment, Mortgage Foreclosure, Receivership, or Judgement proceedings, or any other credit problems during the past ten years? ☐ Yes ☐ No   If yes, please explain on the reverse side.

I hereby certify that the foregoing information is true and accurate to the best of my knowledge and belief.

Date _____   _____
                                  Signature of Buyer

CONFIDENTIAL BUYER QUALIFICATION FORM
(Please Print)

Name _____ Age _____

Spouse _____ Age _____

Address _____ City _____ Zip _____

Number of Dependents _____ Ages _____

Phone { Home _____ / Office _____ }

Financing Desired: VA ☐ FHA ☐ CONV. ☐ OTHER _____

Preferred Down Payment $ _____ Maximum, if needed $ _____

Preferred Monthly Payment $ _____ Maximum, if needed $ _____

Husband	Wife
Employer _____	Employer _____
Address _____	Address _____
Position _____ How Long _____ yrs.	Position _____ How Long _____ yrs.
Average Monthly Income $ _____	Average Monthly Income $ _____

Total Earnings before taxes for last three years:

19 _____ $ _____   19 _____ $ _____   19 _____ $ _____

	Monthly	Yearly
Husband's Income	$ _____	$ _____
Other Income (explain)	$ _____	$ _____
Wife's Income	$ _____	$ _____
Other Income (explain)	$ _____	$ _____
Totals	$ _____	$ _____

Assets		Liabilities	Monthly Payment	Unpaid Balance
Cash	$ _____	Auto	$ _____	$ _____
Stocks, Bonds, etc.	$ _____	Real Estate	$ _____	$ _____
Life Insurance (Cash Value)	$ _____	Loans	$ _____	$ _____
Real Estate	$ _____	Other	$ _____	$ _____
Other	$ _____	Other	$ _____	$ _____
Total	$ _____	Total	$ _____	$ _____

Have you ever been involved in a Bankruptcy, Wage Garnishment, Mortgage Foreclosure, Receivership, or Judgement proceedings, or any other credit problems during the past ten years? ☐ Yes ☐ No If yes, please explain on the reverse side.

I hereby certify that the foregoing information is true and accurate to the best of my knowledge and belief.

Date _____   _____
                                    Signature of Buyer

CONFIDENTIAL BUYER QUALIFICATION FORM
(Please Print)

Name _____ Age _____

Spouse _____ Age _____

Address _____ City _____ Zip _____

Number of Dependents _____ Ages _____

Phone { Home _____

Office _____

Financing Desired: VA ☐ FHA ☐ CONV. ☐ OTHER _____

Preferred Down Payment $ _____ Maximum, if needed $ _____

Preferred Monthly Payment $ _____ Maximum, if needed $ _____

Husband	Wife
Employer _____	Employer _____
Address _____	Address _____
Position _____ How Long _____ yrs.	Position _____ How Long _____ yrs.
Average Monthly Income $ _____	Average Monthly Income $ _____

Total Earnings before taxes for last three years:

19 _____ $ _____   19 _____ $ _____   19 _____ $ _____

	Monthly	Yearly
Husband's Income	$ _____	$ _____
Other Income (explain)	$ _____	$ _____
Wife's Income	$ _____	$ _____
Other Income (explain)	$ _____	$ _____
Totals	$ _____	$ _____

Assets		Liabilities	
		Monthly Payment	Unpaid Balance
Cash . . . . $ _____	Auto . . . . $ _____	$ _____
Stocks, Bonds, etc. . . . . $ _____	Real Estate . . . . . . $ _____	$ _____
Life Insurance (Cash Value) . . . . $ _____	Loans . . . . $ _____	$ _____
Real Estate . . . . $ _____	Other . . . . $ _____	$ _____
Other . . . . $ _____	Other . . . . $ _____	$ _____
Total . . . . $ _____	Total . . . . $ _____	$ _____

Have you ever been involved in a Bankruptcy, Wage Garnishment, Mortgage Foreclosure, Receivership, or Judgement proceedings, or any other credit problems during the past ten years? ☐ Yes ☐ No If yes, please explain on the reverse side.

I hereby certify that the foregoing information is true and accurate to the best of my knowledge and belief.

Date _____   _____

Signature of Buyer

CONFIDENTIAL BUYER QUALIFICATION FORM
(Please Print)

Name _____ Age _____

Spouse _____ Age _____

Address _____ City _____ Zip _____

Number of Dependents _____ Ages _____ Phone { Home _____

Office _____

Financing Desired: VA ☐   FHA ☐   CONV. ☐   OTHER _____

Preferred Down Payment $ _____ Maximum, if needed $ _____

Preferred Monthly Payment $ _____ Maximum, if needed $ _____

Husband	Wife
Employer _____	Employer _____
Address _____	Address _____
Position _____ How Long _____ yrs.	Position _____ How Long _____ yrs.
Average Monthly Income $ _____	Average Monthly Income $ _____

Total Earnings before taxes for last three years:

19 _____ $ _____   19 _____ $ _____   19 _____ $ _____

	Monthly	Yearly
Husband's Income	$ _____	$ _____
Other Income (explain)	$ _____	$ _____
Wife's Income	$ _____	$ _____
Other Income (explain)	$ _____	$ _____
Totals.	$ _____	$ _____

Assets		Liabilities	
		Monthly Payment	Unpaid Balance
Cash. $ _____		Auto. . . . . $ _____	$ _____
Stocks, Bonds, etc. . . . . $ _____		Real Estate. . . . . . $ _____	$ _____
Life Insurance (Cash Value) . . . . $ _____		Loans. . . . . $ _____	$ _____
Real Estate . . . . $ _____		Other . . . . $ _____	$ _____
Other. . . . . $ _____		Other . . . . $ _____	$ _____
Total . . . . $ _____		Total . . . . $ _____	$ _____

Have you ever been involved in a Bankruptcy, Wage Garnishment, Mortgage Foreclosure, Receivership, or Judgement proceedings, or any other credit problems during the past ten years? ☐ Yes ☐ No   If yes, please explain on the reverse side.

I hereby certify that the foregoing information is true and accurate to the best of my knowledge and belief.

Date _____   _____

Signature of Buyer

RECEIPT

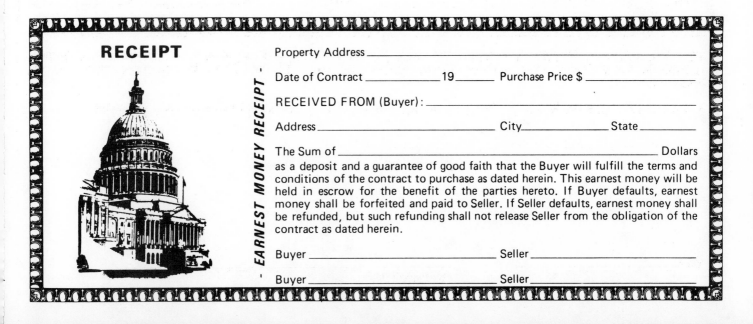

- EARNEST MONEY RECEIPT -

Property Address _____

Date of Contract _____ 19____ Purchase Price $ _____

RECEIVED FROM (Buyer): _____

Address _____ City_____ State_____

The Sum of _____ Dollars
as a deposit and a guarantee of good faith that the Buyer will fulfill the terms and conditions of the contract to purchase as dated herein. This earnest money will be held in escrow for the benefit of the parties hereto. If Buyer defaults, earnest money shall be forfeited and paid to Seller. If Seller defaults, earnest money shall be refunded, but such refunding shall not release Seller from the obligation of the contract as dated herein.

Buyer _____ Seller _____

Buyer _____ Seller _____

RECEIPT

- EARNEST MONEY RECEIPT -

Property Address _____

Date of Contract _____ 19____ Purchase Price $ _____

RECEIVED FROM (Buyer): _____

Address _____ City_____ State_____

The Sum of _____ Dollars
as a deposit and a guarantee of good faith that the Buyer will fulfill the terms and conditions of the contract to purchase as dated herein. This earnest money will be held in escrow for the benefit of the parties hereto. If Buyer defaults, earnest money shall be forfeited and paid to Seller. If Seller defaults, earnest money shall be refunded, but such refunding shall not release Seller from the obligation of the contract as dated herein.

Buyer _____ Seller _____

Buyer _____ Seller _____

RECEIPT

- EARNEST MONEY RECEIPT -

Property Address _____

Date of Contract _____ 19____ Purchase Price $ _____

RECEIVED FROM (Buyer): _____

Address _____ City_____ State_____

The Sum of _____ Dollars
as a deposit and a guarantee of good faith that the Buyer will fulfill the terms and conditions of the contract to purchase as dated herein. This earnest money will be held in escrow for the benefit of the parties hereto. If Buyer defaults, earnest money shall be forfeited and paid to Seller. If Seller defaults, earnest money shall be refunded, but such refunding shall not release Seller from the obligation of the contract as dated herein.

Buyer _____ Seller _____

Buyer _____ Seller _____

SHOWING REGISTER

Owner's Name _____

Address of Property _____

DATE SHOWN	NAME	ADDRESS	TELE. #

SHOWING REGISTER

Owner's Name _____

Address of Property _____

DATE SHOWN	NAME	ADDRESS	TELE. #

HOME INFORMATION FORM
This information is believed reliable, but not warranted.

Address	City	State	Zip	Faces	Rooms	Brms.	Baths	Price
								$

Owner(s)

Phone (Bus.)
Phone (Res.)

Type/Style		Condition — Exc. ☐ Good ☐ Fair ☐
Construction		Electric — 100 amp ☐ 200 amp ☐
Lot Size		Heat cost $
Lot Description		Taxes 19 $
Possession		Gas ☐ Oil ☐ Coal ☐
Age/Builder		Roof Siding
Purchase Year	19	Sewer ☐ Septic ☐
Schools Par.		Water cost $ Well ☐
Schools Pub.	El.	Jr. H.S.

Rooms/Floor	1	2	3	B	Size		
Living						Central Air	
Dining						Carpeting	
Dining Comb. ☐ "L" ☐ Separate ☐						Dishwasher	
Kitchen						Disposal	
Baths						Drapes	
Family Room						Fireplace	
Den						Garage	
Utility Room						Patio	
Mr. Brm.						Porch	
Brm. No. 2						Oven/range Built-in ☐	
Brm. No. 3						Stove	
Brm. No. 4						Storms/screens	
Brm. No. 5						Water Softener ☐ Owned ☐ Rented ☐	

Basement: Full ☐ Partial ☐ Crawl ☐ Slab ☐ Sub-basement ☐ Size:

Other inclusions:

Exclusions:

Directions:

Inspection Procedure: Please Make an Appointment!

Mortgagee:

Mortgage Balance $ P I T I: $ Rate: %   Term: Yrs.

Assumable? Yes ☐ No ☐ If yes — service charge?

Reason for selling:

Remarks:

CUSTOMER ORDER FORM

ANA-DOUG PUBLISHING
4303 N. Bernard, Chicago, Illinois 60618

- All sign panels are constructed from heavy duty 3/16" Duron hardboard and silk screened in two to three colors on both sides with long lasting exterior enamel paints. All posts are constructed of heavy duty tubular steel for rigidity.
- All contracts and riders come in sets of four. The riders must be securely stapled to the contract. Each of the following persons receives one copy: (1) Seller, (2) Buyer, (3) Seller's Attorney and (4) Buyer's Attorney.

QUAN.	ITEM	PRICE	TOTAL
	"Contract To Purchase Real Estate" (4 each)	1.00	
	Rider — "Personal Property Rider" (4 each)	.50	
	Rider — "FHA Appraisal Contingency" (4 each)	.50	
	Rider — "VA Appraisal Contingency" (4 each)	.50	
	Rider — "Contract Contingent On Buyer's Attorney's Approval" (4 each)	.50	
	Rider — "Contract Contingent On Seller's Attorney's Approval" (4 each)	.50	
	Rider — "Contract Contingent On Spouse's Approval" (4 each)	.50	
	Rider — "Contract Contingent On The Sale Of Buyer's Present Home" (4 each)	.50	
	"Confidential Buyer Qualification Form" (4 each)	.50	
	"Home For Sale By Owner" sign, 18" x 24", posts & brackets included	14.95	
	"Open House" sign, 6" x 24", hangs beneath "Home . . ." sign, removable	5.95	
	"Appointment Only" sign, 6" x 24", includes your personal telephone number, hangs beneath "Home . . ." sign, removable	6.95	
	2 "Sold" stickers, 4" x 11"	1.00	
	25 "Open House" cards	1.50	
	The complete "Home For Sale By Owner" KIT, includes every item listed above, a $36.35 value for only . . .	29.95	
	"Home For Sale By Owner" book in the deluxe library edition	14.95	
	3 "Earnest Money Receipts"	.25	
	Free-standing "Open House" sign, 6" x 24", includes post and brackets. If your home is not on a main street, you will need 1 or more extra signs to direct traffic your way.	9.95	
	500 "Home Information Forms," includes typing, layout, and printing	29.95	
	"Real Estate Salesmen Not Welcome!" signs	FREE	XXX

SHIP TO:

Name _____

Address _____

City _____ State _____ Zip _____

Phone Number _____

Total	
Shipping & Handling	
sales tax	
Total Amount Enclosed	

BankAmericard VISA *welcome here*

master charge THE INTERBANK CARD

To order simply fill out the enclosed form and mail it today.

BankAmericard and Master Charge are welcome.

☐ Charge to BankAmericard

☐ Charge to Master Charge

Credit Card No. _____

Use this easy chart to figure postage, insurance, shipping and handling charges.

AMOUNT OF ORDER	Up to 3.00	3.01-5.00	5.01-7.00	7.01-10.00	10.01-15.00	15.01-20.00	20.01-30.00	30.00 & Over
SHIPPING CHARGES	.97	1.24	1.76	2.15	2.68	2.99	3.51	3.92

CUSTOMER ORDER FORM

ANA-DOUG PUBLISHING
4303 N. Bernard, Chicago, Illinois 60618

- All sign panels are constructed from heavy duty 3/16" Duron hardboard and silk screened in two to three colors on both sides with long lasting exterior enamel paints. All posts are constructed of heavy duty tubular steel for rigidity.
- All contracts and riders come in sets of four. The riders must be securely stapled to the contract. Each of the following persons receives one copy: (1) Seller, (2) Buyer, (3) Seller's Attorney and (4) Buyer's Attorney.

QUAN.	ITEM	PRICE	TOTAL
	"Contract To Purchase Real Estate" (4 each)	1.00	
	Rider — "Personal Property Rider" (4 each)	.50	
	Rider — "FHA Appraisal Contingency" (4 each)	.50	
	Rider — "VA Appraisal Contingency" (4 each)	.50	
	Rider — "Contract Contingent On Buyer's Attorney's Approval" (4 each)	.50	
	Rider — "Contract Contingent On Seller's Attorney's Approval" (4 each)	.50	
	Rider — "Contract Contingent On Spouse's Approval" (4 each)	.50	
	Rider — "Contract Contingent On The Sale Of Buyer's Present Home" (4 each)	.50	
	"Confidential Buyer Qualification Form" (4 each)	.50	
	"Home For Sale By Owner" sign, 18" x 24", posts & brackets included	14.95	
	"Open House" sign, 6" x 24", hangs beneath "Home . . ." sign, removable	5.95	
	"Appointment Only" sign, 6" x 24", includes your personal telephone number, hangs beneath "Home . . ." sign, removable	6.95	
	2 "Sold" stickers, 4" x 11"	1.00	
	25 "Open House" cards	1.50	
	The complete "Home For Sale By Owner" KIT, includes every item listed above, a $36.35 value for only . . .	29.95	
	"Home For Sale By Owner" book in the deluxe library edition	14.95	
	3 "Earnest Money Receipts"	.25	
	Free-standing "Open House" sign, 6" x 24", includes post and brackets. If your home is not on a main street, you will need 1 or more extra signs to direct traffic your way.	9.95	
	500 "Home Information Forms," includes typing, layout, and printing	29.95	
	"Real Estate Salesmen Not Welcome!" signs	FREE	XXX

SHIP TO:

Name _____

Address _____

City _____ State _____ Zip _____

Phone Number _____

Total	
Shipping & Handling	
sales tax	
Total Amount Enclosed	

BankAmericard and Master Charge are welcome.

To order simply fill out the enclosed form and mail it today.

☐ Charge to BankAmericard

☐ Charge to Master Charge

Credit Card No. _____

Use this easy chart to figure postage, insurance, shipping and handling charges.

AMOUNT OF ORDER	Up to 3.00	3.01-5.00	5.01-7.00	7.01-10.00	10.01-15.00	15.01-20.00	20.01-30.00	30.00 & Over
SHIPPING CHARGES	.97	1.24	1.76	2.15	2.68	2.99	3.51	3.92